MW01602581

THE CRUSHED Rose

Trusting in God to *Renew* and *Restore* Relationships

SHELLEY K. REICHENBACH

TATE PUBLISHING, LLC

This book is dedicated to my
Lord and Savior Jesus Christ,
In Whom all things are possible.
Matthew 19:26

Thank you Lord Jesus for
embracing, carrying, and never
leaving me through the fiery
trials I have experienced.
Psalms 18:1–3

Acknowledgements

Words cannot express my heartfelt thanks and appreciation to Reverend Donald Grosvenor and his dear wife, Gerri, for their love, prayers, and guidance throughout these many years. They are exceptional examples in their Christian walk. Without their faithfulness in living and delivering the Word of God, this writing would not be one of victory, but most likely just another statistic in the records. It was through the ministry of Pastor Don and Gerri that I learned how to handle the oppositions and struggles of life. Only God knows how many more lives have been salvaged because of their sacrifice and dedication to God's people for over 45 years. They graciously agreed to review my manuscript for scriptural accuracy and context.

I extend sincere thanks to my good friend, Marcena Myhrberg, and my daughter-in-law, Melissa Reichenbach, for their invaluable input and diligent review of my original manuscript.

I cannot say enough about our three wonderful children. During this episode in our lives, they patiently waited and diligently prayed for their troubled parents. Although they did not understand, their love never failed our family. Children are truly a gift from God!

My heart is overwhelmed by having my beloved husband, confidant, and best friend, to be a vital part of this project. I never dreamt of asking him to take on such a task, as there are some painful times interspersed throughout this writing. My husband has not only been supportive, he also agreed to accept the challenge and responsibility to edit this book. I am aware that this project was very hard on my husband, however my heart will forever be grateful that he answered our patient, compassionate Lord Jesus . . . knocking on his heart's door for over 5 years . . . and he came back home. *"Look, I'm standing at the door and knocking. If anyone listens to my voice and opens the door, I'll come in and we'll eat together."* (Revelation 3:20)

The Lord has been so good during this difficult assignment, which He has laid on both of our hearts. In spite of walking through the hellish period in our lives - *together this time* - we have been blessed with God's peace and inspiration. It is our sincere prayer and desire that our experiences in overcoming life's trials through a practical application of the Word of God will minister to those in need.

Contents

Foreword

Any good book must have a story, an author, as well as a message. Unless it is fiction, the story must be true, the author genuine, and the message have an impact. It is my opinion that *The Crushed Rose* has all three of these. This book has a powerful message, from the pen of a woman who is sincerely genuine in her everyday life. I believe Shelley's story will touch every person who chances to read it.

In music, literature, and scripture, great compositions have come out of most unusual experiences. The ability to write about those encounters can provide inspiration to readers of all ages. This was true with King David, Saint Paul, the Apostle John, Abraham Lincoln, Martin Luther, John Wesley, and many others. Their experiences endeared the Lord to them, enabling them to write and share His goodness with others. I believe this is what Shelley has accomplished in this writing.

I have known her for nearly 35 years. I have found her continually to be a loving, compassionate, godly woman who loves people; but even more than people, she loves her God.

May you be blessed - as you share not only her grief - but also her joy in the reality of answered prayer.

Reverend Donald Grosvenor
Founding Pastor
Phoenix Christian Assembly
Phoenix, Arizona

Preface

This writing is for our Lord Jesus Christ, with much prayer and supplication for it to be an encouragement and inspiration to those who need a friend. When there is nowhere else to turn, Jesus is always there patiently waiting. I am sharing my experiences because I feel strongly compelled to do so by Almighty God. There is no doubt in my mind that I was to be an instrument used by God to write a book about my experiences. This book is His project, not mine. He told me from the very beginning of this journey to keep journals and notes. As I look back over these last several years, it is evident to me that this is to be a testimony of God's glory and grace.

This is not a story about the pain endured for a season; instead, it is a story about God's love and the power of His restoration in our lives, marriages, and families. If just one person is saved, or a life is salvaged by applying the Scriptural principles that God has taught me, my spirit will rejoice with the angels in heaven!

I would like to point out that the majority of Scripture quoted in this writing uses the *GOD'S WORD*® translation. This is because it is worded in easy to understand, everyday language, and most importantly, it is accurately translated from the original Hebrew and Greek texts. Visit their website at http://www.godsword.org/home.htm for a thorough explanation of this great work.

The title of this book came to me through the Holy Spirit during a Sunday morning church service. When we think about it, this describes our Lord Jesus. He is the Rose of Sharon, as Solomon tells us in the Song of Solomon 2:1, *"I am a rose of Sharon, a lily [growing] in the valleys."* Roses are lovely, beautiful, and soft with an irresistible aroma. They are often given or received in the spirit of love. Jesus offered love, healing, wisdom, and most of all eternal salvation, but in return, He was crushed, beaten, and bruised, beyond all recognition. Isaiah 53:5 prophetically tells us, *"He was wounded for our rebellious acts. He was crushed for our sins. He was punished so that we could have peace, and we received healing from his wounds."* The King James Version uses the word *bruised,* whereas the *GOD'S WORD®* translation says *crushed.* The original Hebrew word is *dakah*–meaning crushed or shattered. When roses are crushed, their full aroma is released, for all to enjoy. When our Lord Jesus was crushed, His full power and salvation was released for the entire world.

During this time of great trust and spiritual growth, the Lord would lead me from one *room* to another. In explanation, there was a vision of a long, narrow corridor that had a tall dead end, with three doors on each side. These doors were not across from each other, but instead they were staggered and various distances apart. As time progressed, it became apparent that this represented my long journey ahead through different rooms. The unequal distance between doors represented the different amounts of time spent in each room. Each of the first six chapters represents a different room.

He also gave me many other visions and dreams that served to bolster my faith. Several times, *words of prophecy* were given to me one-on-one, while others were to given our whole congregation. I have shared these words of prophecy, dreams, and visions throughout this book, where I felt led by the Holy Spirit, as a testimony to the tender mercies and grace of our Lord Jesus Christ.

Sharing how to defeat Satan and his rulers of darkness through spiritual warfare is the primary focus of this book. (Ephesians 6:11–18) Why live or deal with fearful and unpleasant circumstances or an illness unnecessarily? We have access to the Living Waters that flow from the Throne of God. Step into those waters, asking our Lord for cleansing from all sin, and He will then begin directing your steps through His Word, toward your victory. The omnipotence and faithfulness of our Sovereign God combined with our full commitment to Him is very powerful. We can then rightfully claim and reclaim what is ours! Romans 8:31, *"What can we say about all of this? If God is for us, who can be against us?"*

For twenty years my husband and I, and our three young children lived a committed Christian life through our church, on the job, and in our home. We always tried to keep our ears and hearts open to God's voice. We knew our Lord as a good, merciful, prayer answering God. We served a Sovereign God, one who is in control even when things seem out of control. Our family has always had so much to be thankful for; health, good church family, friends, family, steady employment, increased income, comfortable home, a perfect marriage, and much more. Life was good.

The many years of sitting under the wonderful teaching and preaching of God's word by our beloved Pastor proved to be a life changing experience for my family and me. Little did I know, our family was about to lose it all. God was going to set all happiness and the comforts of life on the shelf for a season. This experience could have so easily destroyed all the members of our family, one by one, for eternity . . . I quickly learned the true meaning of I Peter 5:8, *"Keep your mind clear, and be alert. Your opponent the devil is prowling around like a roaring lion as he looks for someone to devour."*

It is here in my journey that I began to know God in the way described in Philippians 3:9b-10, *" . . . I have God's approval through faith in Christ. This is the approval that comes from God and is based on faith that knows Christ. Faith knows the power that his coming back to life gives and what it means to share his suffering. In this way I'm becoming like him in his death,"* Only when you experience your deepest, most unthinkable fears can you even begin to feel a portion of the pain Jesus suffered . . . for us.

For His Glory,
Shelley K. Reichenbach

Chapter One - Room of Unbelief

The Beginning

My story begins with a successful, perfectly fulfilled 20-year marriage. We were a well-balanced, healthy, and happy family with three beautiful children, pets, and a live-in Grandma. My husband was a successful manager for a manufacturing business, as well as a wonderfully attentive husband and father. I was a teacher at the Christian school that our children attended.

As time passed, the children grew and my husband and I became involved with a business venture. Before we realized it, church attendance was no longer at the top of our priority—we had become too busy . . .

A little over a year passed, and then things grew tenser around our home. It was becoming obvious there were interests that had taken my husband's attention away from our family. I thought that perhaps the business we had agreed to start was having problems, or there was static at the shop. As the weeks passed, this weighed heavily upon my heart. This was not a good sign in the man I knew and loved so very much.

Because the new business required every spare moment and more, there was not enough time for church or family. The mistake of not making time for church services weakens the *natural man*, and our family was no exception. Soon my husband's interests were the pleasures the world had to offer. He was no longer the intimate, compassionate, loving husband I had married. He proceeded to walk in the ways of the world by means of courting another woman. A few weeks later, my husband told me he wanted to start a new life with this woman, which led him to tell me he was not in love with me anymore.

The Language of Tears
It could not be true, because we had the perfect marriage! It took several sleepless weeks and months before reality set in. In the midst of very long, lonely nights, I would often take a drive at one, two, or three a.m. Nothing seemed to matter anymore. I respectfully, but boldly cried to God, "Why, why, why?" This was a question only God could answer.

As each hour of every day passed, I struggled with this new dilemma in my life. I was desperate to find answers. My only source of hope and strength was in God and His Holy Word. Knowing I served a great God, one who I loved dearly, I turned TOTALLY to Him. I began to 'live' in His Word, many hours a day. This is where I found answers to my questions, found hope, and received peace within. Philippians 4:7 tells us, *"Then God's peace, which goes beyond anything we can imagine, will guard your thoughts and emotions through Christ Jesus."* God gave the assurance through His Word that He was in control.

Our Adversary
In I Peter 5:8 we learn, *"Keep your mind clear,*

and be alert. Your opponent the devil is prowling around like a roaring lion as he looks for someone to devour." I soon became aware that our adversary takes great joy in destroying homes, families, and lives. I knew the devil was not only out to destroy our home, he wanted our souls too. His ultimate plan was to turn our hearts against God and take all of us to hell with him for eternity.

The first night I spent alone, the devil clearly let me know he was out to destroy me. In a very real vision, he spoke, "I've got you!" He then vanished. I was extremely shaken. I scrambled for the phone and called my long time Christian friend, telling her everything. She was in disbelief. I then asked her to call our Pastor for me, as I was too distraught. He and his wonderful wife have experienced much heartache along life's pathway. They know and understand the pain, confusion, and fear one can experience at a time such as this. I can say without hesitation that this Pastor and his wife never left my side. Without their faithfulness and example in following God's leading every day in the ministry, this marriage would have had a different outcome.

Now I lost it, absolutely lost it! I fell apart at the foot of the Cross. All anyone could do was pray, as all I could do was pray. I was drowning in a sea of despair, and no one had enough love, hope or faith to save my family . . . it was my nightmare on Elm Street! How could this be happening to a family who served God so faithfully? God was the only One I could turn to . . .

Sin of Unbelief

Hours, days, and weeks passed . . . The reality of this very painful new life did not get any easier - it just got harder. My husband was living his own life and seemed to be doing fine. This was heart wrenching, and watching this transition caused my faith to grow weary. Our adversary, better known as Satan the father of lies, filled my mind with every lie in the book. He tormented me with, "He doesn't love you anymore," or "Can't you see how happy he is?" It seemed to be so true . . . Satan's lies were very difficult to overcome.

Due to the severity of this situation, the unbelief of others was actually hindering God from working. There was a need for frequent prayer and fasting to break the yoke of unbelief in my church family. For unbelief is lack of faith or no faith. God cannot work where there is no faith. Hebrews 11:6 tells us, *"No one can please God without faith. Whoever goes to God must believe that God exists and that he rewards those who seek him."*

Forgiveness

While reading the Word, God led me to I Kings 8:50. *"Forgive your people, who have sinned against you. [Forgive] all their wrongs when they rebelled against you, and cause those who captured them to have mercy on them"* While in church one morning reading this verse, God had laid it on my heart to stand in proxy for my husband, asking God to forgive him for the sins he had committed. This was necessary before God could begin His work. He was also telling me I needed to have a heart that had no malice or condemnation toward anyone. My first thought . . . this was impossible. God said to press into Him and He would miraculously provide His grace and love to accomplish this. To be perfectly frank, I was not at all confident that I could handle this assignment. I don't recall the exact time span, but I struggled with this for a week, perhaps two.

It is here I began to feel a bit like Esther, a woman called of God to save the Jewish people. If Esther had thought only of herself, a nation would have been destroyed. Through my tears and prayers, I kept telling God I was not Esther. The Lord let me know in His omnipotent love and understanding that I did not have to accept this very heavy assignment. However, my plight would be an illness that would cause my life to come to an early end. I believe this would have happened due to a growth in my body that grew noticeably larger every two or three days. God was showing me that He was serious, for it was a matter of eternity.

This broke my heart concerning my children, as I could not let them down, or allow Satan to steal my husband's soul due to my selfish desires. Whatever the cost, I had to submit fully to God with a broken heart. The Holy Spirit gently reminded me of I Corinthians 10:13, *"There isn't any temptation that you have experienced which is unusual for humans. God, who faithfully keeps his promises, will not allow you to be tempted beyond your power to resist. But when you are tempted, he will also give you the ability to endure the temptation as your way of escape."*

I followed this commandment throughout each day. After some time, by God's infinite grace and power, I had let go of much of my selfish desires and replaced them with God's desires. The victory would be won through God's divine power and wisdom, not mine.

I was frequently reminded of what Jesus prayed at Gethsemane, as recorded in Luke 22:42, *"Father, if it is your will, take this cup [of suffering] away from me. However, your will must be done, not mine."* I had nothing to complain about when I thought of what Jesus was called to do. Meditating upon this gave me strength in my spirit, and courage to face another day.

I then realized that time was of the essence, and there was a war to be won. This war would not be fought with people and their differences, but with the enemy of our souls. God gave me Psalms 32:7–8, *"You are my hiding place. You protect me from trouble. You surround me with joyous songs of salvation. Selah [The LORD says,] "I will instruct you. I will teach you the way that you should go. I will advise you as my eyes watch over you."* This part of my journey lasted approximately six months.

Dealing with Anger

Before we move on to the next chapter, I am sure that you are wondering how I dealt with my anger and frustration. Psalms 139:14–16 declares, *"I will give thanks to you because I have been so amazingly and miraculously made. Your works are miraculous, and my soul is fully aware of this. My bones were not hidden from you when I was being made in secret, when I was being skillfully woven in an underground workshop. Your eyes saw me when I was only a fetus. Every day [of my life] was recorded in your book before one of them had taken place."*

How true, the adult human body consists of 206 bones and over 600 muscles. In addition, our Maker has given each one of us emotions, and a free will. Of the many emotions God gave us, anger is probably the most difficult to control. Webster's dictionary defines anger as 'showing vexation, hot resentment, wrath, or rage.' How well we know, and realize that the results of an outburst can cause irreparable damage. Yet we are human, and can only tolerate so much. I knew down deep in my heart that if I said what I wanted, expressing myself, I would be interfering with God's plans of restoring my marriage . . . let alone my husband's salvation. (Family)

In dealing with my anger, I did not want to continue wearing my wedding ring. I dearly loved my ring, but it no longer represented the perfect marriage. Each time that I looked at it, I was reminded of what I no longer possessed. As I struggled with this, I tried removing my ring just once trying to make life a little easier. I was quickly rebuked by the Holy Spirit. What kind of faith is that for one who believed in her marriage? I put it back on right away; it never came off again.

I tried putting myself in my husband's shoes. Would I want to be a Christian, if one who claimed to be a dedicated Christian, acted out in anger toward me? This is why I needed to have the mind of Christ every moment of each day. I was very aware that I couldn't let my words fly out in anger, hurt and frustration. This was extremely difficult, as I believed that I was justified in being angry. I thought I had the right to put my Christianity aside for a moment and give my husband a piece of my mind . . . everyone else does, right?

Once again, I was immediately rebuked in my spirit for thinking only of myself. This was not about me . . . At these times, I spent much time in fasting and prayer. While pouring out my heart before God, He would gently remind me this battle was for my beloved's soul. Many times, I felt like a casualty of war. During my time with the Lord, I would ask Him to give me a specific passage or Scripture for my need. After periods of crying, praying, and waiting on God, I would read and study Scriptures as I felt led. Jehovah-Rapha, The Lord my Healer, always put me back together one more time, for one more day.

In my studies, I learned that God has much to say about anger. The following passages are full of His truth and wisdom!

- Psalms 37:8, *"Let go of anger, and leave rage behind. Do not be preoccupied. It only leads to evil."*
- Proverbs 29:22–23, *"An angry person stirs up a fight, and a hothead does much wrong. A person's pride will humiliate him, but a humble spirit gains honor."*
- Proverbs 22:24–25, *"Do not be a friend of one who has a bad temper, and never keep com-*

pany with a hothead, or you will learn his ways and set a trap for yourself."

- Proverbs 19:11, *"A person with good sense is patient, and it is to his credit that he overlooks an offense."* This passage hit me right between the eyes!

I tell you that ONLY by His grace could I accomplish II Corinthians 12:9, *"But he told me: "My kindness is all you need. My power is strongest when you are weak." So I will brag even more about my weaknesses in order that Christ's power will live in me."* In James 1:19–20 we learn, *"Remember this, my dear brothers and sisters: Everyone should be quick to listen, slow to speak, and should not get angry easily. An angry person doesn't do what God approves of."*

To sum up my angry feelings . . . I was totally incapable of handling my anger on my own. Unsure of my ability to follow this tall order, I pleaded before God for every ounce of strength that He would impart to me. Looking back, it is obvious to me that the only way I made it through was by the tender mercies and grace of my awesome Lord and Savior, Jesus Christ.

Chapter Two - Room of Promises and Prayer

The First Promise

It was time to press into God in a way I had never done before. I searched the Scriptures for answers. God always promises to answer our cries. He led me to Isaiah 30:18–21: *"The LORD is waiting to be kind to you. He rises to have compassion on you. The LORD is a God of justice. Blessed are all those who wait for him. You will live in Zion, in Jerusalem. You won't cry anymore. The LORD will certainly have pity on you when you cry for help. As soon as he hears you, he will answer you. The Lord may give you troubles and hardships. But your teacher will no longer be hidden from you. You will see your teacher with your own eyes. You will hear a voice behind you saying, "This is the way. Follow it, whether it turns to the right or to the left."* In this passage, the Lord let me know that He knew exactly where I was, and understood all of my fears, yet assured me He would take care of me through it all.

God also gave me Isaiah 54:5–7, stating it very clearly; *"Your husband is your maker. His name is the LORD of Armies. Your defender is the Holy One of Israel. He is called the God of the whole earth. "The LORD has called you as if you were a wife who was abandoned and in grief, a wife who married young and was rejected," says your God. "I abandoned you for one brief moment, but I will bring you back with unlimited compassion."* Through the Word, God let me know up front this journey was going to be the most difficult situation I had ever encountered. However, it was all in His plan for my life. My job was to hold tight to His hand and not waiver in my faith. God had given me the *scoop*. It was not going to be easy, but I had to obey. The Lord assured me He was in charge and that His grace and compassion would be with me all the way.

It was revealed to me that this was not a battle to save my marriage; rather it was a spiritual battle regarding my husband's soul. I knew when the enemy showed himself to me on that first night, he was after the souls of my family members.

However, God also gave the promise of restoration in my marriage in Isaiah 62:4–8. *"You will no longer be called Deserted, and your land will no longer be called Destroyed. But you will be named My Delight, and your land will be named Married. The LORD is delighted with you, and your land will be married. As a young man marries a woman, so your sons will marry you. As a bridegroom rejoices over his bride, so your God will rejoice over you. I have posted watchmen on your walls, Jerusalem. They will never be silent day or night. Whoever calls on the LORD, do not give yourselves any rest, and do not give him any rest until he establishes Jerusalem and makes it an object of praise throughout the earth. The LORD has sworn with his right hand and with his mighty arm, "I will never again let your enemies eat your grain, nor will foreigners drink the new wine which you made."* God tells me here He would not rest until this was done! WOW! I clung to that promise for the duration of our separation.

Another fantastic promise! His Word will not return void, or until the job is finished. The prophet Isaiah proclaims in Chapter 55, verse 11, *"My word, which comes from my mouth, is like the rain and snow. It will not come back to me without results. It will accomplish whatever I want and achieve whatever I send it to do."* Throughout my journey, I stood on this promise as well.

My friend of many years was more familiar with God's Word and promises than was I at this point in my Christian walk. She was raised in a dedicated born-again Christian family. She was sold out to God, allowing Him to use her and her family. I believe that I would not have experienced God's deep, passionate love without the support of my friend. I was unable to carry this cross by myself at this time. Through this experience, I learned obedience was better than sacrifice as found in I Samuel 15:22. *"Then Samuel said, "Is the LORD as delighted with burnt offerings and sacrifices as he would be with your obedience? To follow instructions is better than to sacrifice. To obey is better than sacrificing the fat of rams."*

I became an avid reader of the Bible to build my faith and to seek instruction from the Lord. Through my readings in the beginning of this most difficult time, my faith began to grow, as the Lord would speak to me through His Word. Isaiah 55:8–9 says, *"My thoughts are not your thoughts, and my ways are not your ways,"* declares the LORD. *"Just as the heavens are higher than the earth, so my ways are higher than your ways, and my thoughts are higher than your thoughts."* This calmed me in extreme times of fear and confusion. There were countless times I had ONLY God and His Word, PERIOD. Continuing to read the 55th Chapter of Isaiah, I received much encouragement. Due to this, I found myself studying my Bible three to four times daily. It fed me . . . empowering me . . . to face each new day.

I learned that using the right tools of faith, combined with obedience to God, I could have everything back, and even more, than the enemy had taken from me. One of the first clues that God planned to restore my family was found in Matthew 21:21–22. *"Jesus answered them, "I can guarantee this truth: If you have faith and do not doubt, you will be able to do what I did to the fig tree. You could also say to this mountain, 'Be uprooted and thrown into the sea,' and it will happen. Have faith that you will receive whatever you ask for in prayer."* Little by little, my friend encouraged me to take back what the enemy had stolen, by FAITH ALONE. Until His promises were manifested in my life, God instructed me that He would be all I would ever need.

I had to trust God, knowing and understanding that He was in control. He is the Sovereign God of the Universe, which meant I should not panic. Well, I did . . . many times . . . However, He would always calm me through prayer, singing, and reading Scripture. I resolved to stay in the Word, as that was the only place I found peace, hope, and instruction. Another beautiful promise is in Isaiah 30:15a, *"This is what the Almighty LORD, the Holy One of Israel, says: You can be saved by returning to me. You can have rest. You can be strong by being quiet and by trusting me . . ."*

Benefits of a Broken Heart

As I studied the Word, the Lord continued to lead me into things that are difficult for the carnal mind to understand. To become solely dependent on the Lord in life, we must yield to the Holy Spirit, allowing Him to change our hearts to become like our Lord Jesus. *"The LORD is near to those whose hearts are humble. He saves those whose spirits are crushed. The righteous person has many troubles, but the LORD rescues him from all of them."* (Psalms 34:18–19) Another translation that I like very much tells us, *"The LORD is nigh unto them that are of a broken heart; and saveth such as be of a contrite spirit. Many are the afflictions of the righteous: but the LORD delivereth him out of them all."* (KJV) To be contrite means to be humble and penitent. This is pleasing and acceptable to God, as it draws us closer to Him. Spiritually speaking, God wants and desires a heart that is humble and penitent. This takes place as we give God more of our very being and allow Him to become the center of our lives and He becomes the reason we live.

"You are extremely happy about these things, even though you have to suffer different kinds of trouble for a little while now. The purpose of these troubles is to test your faith as fire tests how genuine gold is. Your faith is more precious than gold, and

by passing the test, it gives praise, glory, and honor to God. This will happen when Jesus Christ appears again. Although you have never seen Christ, you love him. You don't see him now, but you believe in him. You are extremely happy with joy and praise that can hardly be expressed in words as you obtain the salvation that is the goal of your faith." In John 3:30, we are told, *"He must increase in importance, while I must decrease in importance."* (I Peter 1:6–9)

This humbling process is painful for a time. However, the benefits are priceless, for they are with you to your journey's end. The Word teaches us how to pray for God's perfect will, rather than our own selfish desires. Each morning I learned to commit myself to His perfect will, praying for the mind of Christ, I Corinthians 2:16 teaches us, *"Who has known the mind of the Lord so that he can teach him?" However, we have the mind of Christ."* We also read in Romans 12:1–2, *"Brothers and sisters, in view of all we have just shared about God's compassion, I encourage you to offer your bodies as living sacrifices, dedicated to God and pleasing to him. This kind of worship is appropriate for you. Don't become like the people of this world. Instead, change the way you think. Then you will always be able to determine what God really wants—what is good, pleasing, and perfect."*

According to this Scripture, it is our solemn duty and responsibility as Christians to present ourselves as living sacrifices to the Lord each day. If we neglect to do this on any given day, this Scripture tells us we won't know God's will when a situation arises.

We have no guarantee that we will not make a poor decision or speak foolish or unkind words to one in need. We could easily give place to the devil, giving him the opportunity to cause havoc in our lives, or in the lives of others. We need the mind of Christ to live each day as Christians, thinking of others before ourselves, and living above circumstances. This way, we think like Jesus . . . because we have committed our thoughts and actions to Him. Therefore, we have the tendency to be more like Christ, rather than our doubtful or prideful selves.

Power of Words

Watch the words that you speak! Job 15:5–6 warns us; *"Your sin teaches you what to say. You choose [to talk with] a sly tongue. Your [own] mouth condemns you, not I. Your lips testify against you."* As we speak His Word, we are promised in Revelation 12:11–12 that we are victorious by our words! *"They overcame him by the blood of the Lamb and by the word of their testimony; they did not love their lives so much as to shrink from death. Therefore rejoice, you heavens and you who dwell in them! But woe to the earth and the sea, because the devil has gone down to you! He is filled with fury, because he knows that his time is short."* (NIV) We also read that as we practice doing God's will, our fears and frustrations will be replaced by God's peace. *"Those who live by the corrupt nature have the corrupt nature's attitude. But those who live by the spiritual nature have the spiritual nature's attitude. The corrupt nature's attitude leads to death. But the spiritual nature's atti-*

tude leads to life and peace. This is so because the corrupt nature has a hostile attitude toward God. It refuses to place itself under the authority of God's standards because it can't. Those who are under the control of the corrupt nature can't please God. But if God's Spirit lives in you, you are under the control of your spiritual nature, not your corrupt nature. Whoever doesn't have the Spirit of Christ doesn't belong to him." (Romans 8:5–9) We all function better when we are not consumed by circumstances. We must make a difference as Christians. The only way we can make a difference is with Jesus living in us. It is truly imperative that we commit our ways to the Lord and pray . . . each day.

During these times of prayer in the morning, God spoke to the depths of my soul, telling me that I must lay my husband as well as my marriage, in its entirety, on the altar. I had to leave it there and walk away . . . It was *let go and let God*. This was like going back to day one all over again. I truly could not understand at the time why God would ask me to lay my marriage down, as He was the creator of the marriage union. Once again, I had a most difficult task before me. I struggled with walking through this very sad, fiery trial with the possibility of no restoration brought to our marriage after all.

Jesus wanted to be Number One in my life. I came to realize that He was not, as my husband had occupied that spot for the last 20 years. I was reminded that this was not about me, or my present pain, but rather about my husband's soul. How could I turn my back on God's request and rob the man I loved of an eternity with our Lord and Savior, Jesus Christ. I began to seek God in an even greater way. I opened God's Word looking for anything that would help me. The Holy Spirit gently kneaded the Word of God into the depths of my fearful heart. My Bible fell open to Matthew 6:33–34, *"But first, be concerned about his kingdom and what has His approval. Then all these things will be provided for you. So don't ever worry about tomorrow. After all, tomorrow will worry about itself. Each day has enough trouble of its own."* The Lord also reassured me in Isaiah 26:3–4, *"With perfect peace you will protect those whose minds cannot be changed, because they trust you. Trust the LORD always, because the LORD, the LORD alone, is an everlasting rock."* Knowing that I desired to please God, I continued on this journey holding tightly to His hand giving Him full control of my husband, my marriage, my life . . ."*We were saved with this hope in mind. If we hope for something we already see, it's not really hope. Who hopes for what can be seen? But if we hope for what we don't see, we eagerly wait for it with perseverance."* (Romans 8:24–25)

In His Presence

To begin each day, the Lord prepares us to face the required tasks our day may hold. I highly recommend that you commit the following passages to heart.

- *"Splendor and majesty are in his presence. Strength and joy are where he is."* (I Chronicles 16:27)

- *"Let's come into his presence with a song of thanksgiving. Let's shout happily to him with psalms."* (Psalms 95:2)
- *"Serve the LORD cheerfully. Come into his presence with a joyful song."* (Psalms 100:2)

It is here we find the commandment to come into the presence of the Lord and serve the Lord with gladness. We will find strength, joy, wisdom, grace, and healing in the presence of the Lord. Our God is a God of restoration. You will be refreshed and rejuvenated while spending time in His presence. In addition, fear is dispelled, or driven away by the presence of God.

Attempting to deal with circumstances of life in your own strength will only wear you down. You will more than likely become discouraged and possibly make wrong decisions because of life's distractions. On the mornings I ran late, not taking time before the Lord, my day was noticeably more difficult. I did not have the patience or compassion I normally had, and I was exhausted by 2:00 p.m. I still had several hours before my day would slow down. I did not take what God offered me, like my daily vitamins, to face the world. I was not renewed, therefore, I was not refreshed. I learned the hard way . . . TAKE THE TIME . . . If you have to sacrifice a few minutes here and there, you will be glad you did! Even today, on days when I am overtired or not feeling well, I find myself drawn to spend time in His presence. A few moments in His presence will restore, refresh, and renew . . . physically, emotionally, and spiritually.

In Psalms 39:7–12, we read that David does not question Almighty God in the midst of trouble. *"And now, Lord, what am I waiting for? My hope is in you! Rescue me from all my rebellious acts. Do not disgrace me in front of godless fools. I remained speechless. I did not open my mouth because you are the one who has done this. Remove the sickness you laid upon me. My life is over because you struck me with your hand. With stern warnings you discipline people for their crimes. Like a moth you eat away at what is dear to them. Certainly, everyone is like a whisper in the wind. Selah Listen to my prayer, O LORD. Open your ear to my cry for help. Do not be deaf to my tears, for I am a foreign resident with you, a stranger like all my ancestors."* David also leaves us a good example in Psalms 27:4–6, *"I have asked one thing from the LORD. This I will seek: to remain in the LORD's house all the days of my life in order to gaze at the LORD's beauty and to search for an answer in his temple. He hides me in his shelter when there is trouble. He keeps me hidden in his tent. He sets me high on a rock. Now my head will be raised above my enemies who surround me. I will offer sacrifices with shouts of joy in his tent. I will sing and make music to praise the LORD."*

God never promised us a perfect childhood, followed by health, happiness, and prosperity. However, He does promise that His grace is sufficient for any and all our needs.

- The Apostle Paul tells us in II Corinthians 12:9, *"But he told me: "My kindness is all you need.*

*My power is strongest when you are weak." So
I will brag even more about my weaknesses in
order that Christ's power will live in me."*

- He also promises in II Timothy 2:11–12, *"This
is a statement that can be trusted: If we have
died with him, we will live with him. If we
endure, we will rule with him. If we disown
him, he will disown us."*

- And, in Philippians 4:19, *"My God will richly
fill your every need in a glorious way through
Christ Jesus."*

We can receive His grace, and an extra dose
of faith in His presence. These are extremely powerful verses. God answered my prayers, encouraged
my heart, and strengthened my hope and faith in His
ability to perform miracles.

My prayer continues to be Psalms 19:14, *"May
the words of my mouth and the meditation of my heart
be pleasing in your sight, O LORD, my Rock and my
Redeemer."* (NIV)

God's Holiness

The biblical view of God's Holiness refers to
His character as absolute, total good, and entirely
without evil. A classic text on God's Holiness is
found in Isaiah 6:1–9. He also tells us in Leviticus
11:44–45, *"Here is the reason: I am the LORD your
God. You must live holy lives. Be holy because I am
holy. Never become unclean by touching anything
that swarms or crawls on the ground. Here is the
reason [again]: I am the LORD. I brought you out of*

Egypt to be your God. Be holy because I am holy."
I can see Romans 12:1–2 in this passage. Oh, how I
wish people really knew our God, He is so good, but
people do not give Him a chance!

According to I Samuel 2:2, God's Holiness
displays strength, and His uniqueness is like no other
being! *"There is no one holy like the LORD. There is
no one but you, O LORD. There is no Rock like our
God."* There is absolutely nothing in this universe
to compare to Him! We have nothing like divine
holiness. It stands apart, unapproachable, incom-
prehensible, and unattainable to the natural man. To
be holy is not conforming to a standard, He is the
Standard, period. The attributes of our Holy God are
His Holiness, Justice, Mercy, Love, and Truth. God
sent His only Begotten Son for us, the manifestation
of His love. Because God is Holy, He is above the
imperfections of all of His creations. Therefore, He
is able to deliver His people! He is more than worthy
of our praise!

In consideration of all that I have shared with
you in the last few pages about praise and worship,
remember, life goes on. God's plan for our lives is
always to live above circumstances and walk in victory. He has given us the tools to do so, however, it is
not always easy. God wants us to fight the devil, *"He
trains my hands for battle, So that my arms can bend
a bow of bronze. You have also given me the shield of
Your salvation, And Your right hand upholds me; And
Your gentleness makes me great."* (Psalms 18:34–35
NASB) We have to fight! Do not sit and watch the
devil destroy your marriage, health, children, loved

ones, finances, or anything else . . . Start now, and take back the things the devil has robbed from you! We serve a God of restoration. Remember, it is necessary to spend time with God and in His Word every day to be victorious.

"Those who cry while they plant will joyfully sing while they harvest. The person who goes out weeping, carrying his bag of seed, will come home singing, carrying his bundles of grain." (Psalms 126:5–6) This is where I found my strength to continue and not let go of God's hand.

Spiritual Weapons of Warfare

I diligently continued to seek God daily on forgiving my husband and the other woman. I knew God could not do His work if there was iniquity in my heart. I began reading I Kings 8:50 aloud, and worshipping God with songs, hymns, and spiritual songs. The Apostle Paul in Colossians 3:16 exhorts us, *"Let Christ's word with all its wisdom and richness live in you. Use psalms, hymns, and spiritual songs to teach and instruct yourselves about [God's] kindness. Sing to God in your hearts."*

In Proverbs Chapter 31, we read about a virtuous woman. The Hebrew translation for virtuous is mighty, or strong. God intends for the woman to be the fighter, a prayer warrior for her husband, children, family . . .

I must now turn aside from my story to share some of God's *strong meat* of the Word with you. This section of the book will help you prepare to take back what the enemy has robbed from you. In dealing with our adversary Satan, I have learned much about how to use the weapons of warfare that our Lord has given us. Natural deeds, works, and thoughts are powerless against the devil. That is why the natural solution to problems will not work. We need a spiritual solution to a spiritual problem, just as we need an antibiotic to fight an infection. I recommend that you have your Bible available to study the Scripture references given. May our Heavenly Father enlighten you as you read what He has put upon my heart. Paul tells us in Galatians 5:16–17, *"Let me explain further. Live your life as your spiritual nature directs you. Then you will never follow through on what your corrupt nature wants. What your corrupt nature wants is contrary to what your spiritual nature wants, and what your spiritual nature wants is contrary to what your corrupt nature wants. They are opposed to each other. As a result, you don't always do what you intend to do."*

Names of God

There are many Hebrew names and titles for our LORD God. These are the ones that daily speak to my heart. NOTE: To address the different attributes of our LORD, the titles of Jehovah and Adonai are normally combined with other names, while the title of Adonai may be used by itself. After reading and studying these Names of God, we have no reason to doubt that He is capable of meeting our every need . . . JUST BELIEVE!

• Jehovah-M'Kaddesh, The LORD Who Makes

Holy: (Ezekiel 37:28). He is holy, unique, special, one of a kind. There is one God and there is no one and nothing like Him. The closer we get to Him, the holier we become.

- Jehovah-Jireh, The LORD Will Provide. (Genesis 22:1–18) He is all seeing and is aware of our problems and needs. The LORD is committed to providing for all the needs of His people.

- Jehovah-Nissi, The LORD My Miracle, or The LORD My Banner. (Exodus 17:11–16). If we need a miracle, Adonai is able to perform one for us. He is our banner or standard. In the midst of life's raging battles, He is high and lifted up. If we keep our eyes on Him, and follow Him, we will be miraculously victorious.

- Jehovah-Shalom, The LORD of Peace. (Judges 6:24). Shalom means completeness and peace. The LORD is complete in and of Himself. He needs nothing to add to His completeness.

- Jehovah-Tzidkenu, The LORD Our Righteousness. (Jeremiah 23:6, 33:16). The LORD is perfectly right and just in all that He says and does. Entering into a personal faith relationship with Adonai is what makes us right. Righteousness does not come by keeping commandments or doing good deeds, but by having a right relationship with Him, and being declared righteous by Him.

- Jehovah-Rapha, The LORD Your Healer. (Exodus 15:22–26). He is the Great Physician and the ultimate source of all healing, spiritual and physical. If you are in need of any kind of healing, He is the first One to turn to.

• Jehovah-Osenu, The LORD Our Maker. (Psalms 95:6). The LORD is our Creator. Since He is our Maker, He deserves all that we have and all that we are.

Our Armor from God

We are told in Ephesians 6:11–18, *"Put on all the armor that God supplies. In this way you can take a stand against the devil's strategies. This is not a wrestling match against a human opponent. We are wrestling with rulers, authorities, the powers who govern this world of darkness, and spiritual forces that control evil in the heavenly world. For this reason, take up all the armor that God supplies. Then you will be able to take a stand during these evil days. Once you have overcome all obstacles, you will be able to stand your ground. So then, take your stand! Fasten truth around your waist like a belt. Put on God's approval as your breastplate. Put on your shoes so that you are ready to spread the Good News that gives peace. In addition to all these, take the Christian faith as your shield. With it you can put out all the flaming arrows of the evil one. Also take salvation as your helmet and the Word of God as the sword that the Spirit supplies. Pray in the Spirit in every situation. Use every kind of prayer and request there is. For the same reason be alert. Use every kind of effort and make every kind of request for all of God's people."*

Spiritual warfare is necessary to loosen people

or situations from Satan's grip. Spiritual strength and courage are needed for our spiritual warfare. The armor God provides for His people is to be worn every day. You cannot fight the devil without it. Those who do spiritual warfare must put on the whole armor of God, because it protects us from the darts the devil throws. It is to be worn until our warfare is complete. We will know in our spirit when that time has come.

We must remember that we are not fighting people, so we must not lose the focus of the true battle. *"The weapons we use in our fight are not made by humans. Rather, they are powerful weapons from God. With them we destroy people's defenses, that is, their arguments and all their intellectual arrogance that oppose the knowledge of God. We take every thought captive so that it is obedient to Christ."* (II Corinthians 10:4–5) The devil is always trying to distract God's people from the real battle that he has thrown our way. We must resolve by God's grace and power, not to yield to Satan. Resist him, and he will flee, as we are told in James 4:7. *"So place yourselves under God's authority. Resist the devil, and he will run away from you."* If we give way, the devil will gain ground, and if we lack faith, we have given him a distinct advantage.

The righteousness of Christ imparted in us fortifies our hearts against the attacks of Satan. During the times of trial, our motives must be pure; drawn from a clear knowledge of the Gospel. As we apply faith, we are applying the Word of God and the grace of Christ . . . this is what quenches the darts. The Sword of the Spirit, which is the Word of God, subdues evil desires, unbelief, and wrong thoughts, as they rise within our minds. Our thoughts, works, and deeds must be from a pure heart. A vain heart will be vain in prayer. We must pray with all the parts of prayer. Acknowledge His Holiness and that His will be done, confession of sin, petition for mercy, and thanksgiving for favors received. The example Jesus taught us is in Matthew 6:9–13, *"This is how you should pray: Our Father in heaven, let your name be kept holy. Let your kingdom come. Let your will be done on earth as it is done in heaven. Give us our daily bread today. Forgive us as we forgive others. Don't allow us to be tempted. Instead, rescue us from the evil one."* He ended His teaching on prayer with this warning in verses 14 and 15, *"If you forgive the failures of others, your heavenly Father will also forgive you. But if you don't forgive others, your Father will not forgive your failures."*

We must do it by the grace of God, and the Holy Spirit. We must pray, not for ourselves only, but for all our brothers and sisters in Christ, here and abroad. Our enemies are evil and strong, but in the power of God's might and the weapons of warfare, we can overcome. Prayer moves the hand of God!

Power of the Blood

Blood is a strange substance. The Bible does not tell us the chemical composition of the blood, yet the Bible indicates that the life is in the blood. Leviticus 17:11 states, *" . . . because blood contains life. I have given this blood to you to make peace with me on the altar. Blood is needed to make peace with me."*

In Psalms 139:14, we read, *"I will give thanks to you because I have been so amazingly and miraculously made. Your works are miraculous, and my soul is fully aware of this."* We are far more wonderfully made than even angels are. Never underestimate the power of the blood! When you apply the Blood of Jesus to a situation by faith, Satan will flee because the Blood of Jesus is alive. The life is in the blood. The devil hates the mention of the Blood of Jesus. Many times by speaking it, I have covered mine, or my children's eyes, ears, and mouth with the Blood of Jesus. This is saying we want to see, hear, and speak the things that Jesus would desire of us. Pleading the Blood MUST be prayed in the Name of Jesus, or the words hold no power.

As soon as a Christian speaks the precious Blood of Jesus over anything, anyone, or any situation, the devil trembles. The devil understands the power of the Blood of Jesus, and has done everything possible to blind Christians to this truth. It is only faith in the Blood of Jesus that comes between us, and the devil with his demon hordes. If you have faith that the Blood of Jesus covers your home and family, it will! Animals have even been healed by the laying on of hands through faith and pleading the Blood of Jesus over them. It is very important to speak your words of faith audibly and to plead the Blood aloud! The devil hears you and flees! As Christians, we possess the most powerful weapon in the Universe. We need only to appropriate it to defeat the forces of darkness!

Because the enemy is stubborn, the victory

does not always come quickly. Sometimes we battle by pleading the Blood in prayer for weeks or months, but victory is certain! Revelation 12:11 says, *"They won the victory over him because of the blood of the lamb and the word of their testimony. They didn't love their life so much that they refused to give it up."* Peace of mind and wonderful answers to prayers come to those who practice the covering of the Blood over their family, home, and circumstances on a daily basis. Satan cannot step across the Blood of Jesus, UNLESS there is disobedience or unbelief in the one who is praying this prayer. The Blood is a vital part of faith!

An army without weapons is defeated before ever engaging in battle. We are no exception . . . the Army of the Lord is powerless until we use the weapons made available to us. They are the Sword of the Spirit, which is the Word of God, and the Blood. These weapons are mighty in bringing down strongholds that are causing turmoil in our lives. If every Christian would plead the Blood of Jesus daily, ALOUD, the result would be that Satan's kingdom would be shaken to the core. Our churches, as well as our nation, would receive showers of blessing from our Lord God that would be astonishing!

Prayer, praise, and worship are all a part of spiritual warfare, but *speaking aloud* the Blood of Jesus through faith will bring wonderful results. By doing this, you are reminding God that you trust Him.

Power of Prayer
What a privilege to carry everything to the Lord

in prayer! Before we begin to speak, Jesus hears us. Isaiah 65:24 says, *"Before they call, I will answer. While they're still speaking, I will hear."* To pray is to give Jesus permission to handle our troubles. The Psalms frequently refer to praying as crying, lifting up the eyes, and lifting up the soul. Not only is praying a privilege, but it is an obligation according to Jesus, as recorded in Luke 18:1. *"Jesus used this illustration with his disciples to show them that they need to pray all the time and never give up."*

Prayer is allowing God to work through you. Jesus separated Himself many times from people in order to pray. Prayer was more important to Jesus than His teaching and healing ministry. Philippians 4:6 tells us, *"Never worry about anything. But in every situation let God know what you need in prayers and requests while giving thanks."* Jeremiah proclaims in Chapter 33, verse 3, *"Call to me, and I will answer you. I will tell you great and mysterious things that you do not know."*

Through the preaching and teaching of my Pastor, I learned that praise and worship were very effective tools for spiritual warfare. James 2:19 says, *"You believe that there is one God. That's fine! The demons also believe that, and they tremble with fear."* Satan and his demons run at the sound of praise and worship. I learned to worship when frightened, discouraged, lonely, or just not knowing which way to turn.

Praying became a full time job, as well as a full time desire. I discovered that I found great comfort and strength after spending time in prayer. The load is much lighter after we leave our burdens at the foot of the Cross. II Corinthians 10:4–5 bears repeating . . ."*The weapons we use in our fight are not made by humans. Rather, they are powerful weapons from God. With them we destroy people's defenses, that is, their arguments and all their intellectual arrogance that oppose the knowledge of God. We take every thought captive so that it is obedient to Christ."* Paul exhorts us in Ephesians 5:18b-20, " . . . *Instead, be filled with the Spirit, by reciting psalms, hymns, and spiritual songs for your own good. Sing and make music to the Lord with your hearts. Always thank God the Father for everything in the name of our Lord Jesus Christ."* This was the *recipe* God Almighty gave me in order to win the victory in this war. God revealed to me that the victory would come through worship and singing His praises THROUGHOUT this journey, just as He instructed Jehoshaphat in II Chronicles 20:21–22. *"After he had advised the people, he appointed people to sing to the LORD and praise him for the beauty of his holiness. As they went in front of the troops, they sang, "Thank the LORD because his mercy endures forever!" As they started to sing praises, the LORD set ambushes against the Ammonites, Moabites, and the people of Mount Seir who had come into Judah. They were defeated."*

This was His war as He tells us II Chronicles 32:8a, *"The king of Assyria has human power on his side, but the LORD our God is on our side to help us and fight our battles . . ."* Prayer is always good, as it keeps us in contact with our Lord and Savior. *"As soon as you began to make your request, a reply was sent. I have come to give you the reply because you are highly respected. So study the message, and understand the vision."* (Daniel 9:23) What an awesome God we serve! Prayer is so powerful! We must be diligent and mindful of this at all times, staying alert and always praying for the saints of God. In Ephesians 6:19, the Apostle Paul speaks, *"Also pray that God will give me the right words to say. Then I will speak boldly when I reveal the mystery of the Good News."*

If you believe God is leading you in the way of spiritual warfare regarding a situation, be prepared for opposition from the enemy. Make sure you put on the full armor of God as explained at the beginning of this chapter. (Ephesians 6:11–18)

Seriously consider these items before you gird for battle:

- Be holy and remain holy before Almighty God.
- Recognize your adversary.
- Learn his strategies.
- Never lose sight of your Eternal Purpose.
- Be wise and vigilant, yet harmless as a dove.
- Daily feed your spirit through the Word.
- Do not forsake the assembling of the brethren, stay in church.
- Know your weapons and use them.
- Avoid appearance of wrongdoing, remain pure.
- Fear nothing.
- Do not compromise or contradict God's Word.

- Do not look at the natural life, God works in the spiritual realm.
- Never lay down your armor.
- Reflect Christ in your life.
- Remember God does not live by a clock, answers take time, *and He is never late.*

God's Battle

God continued to lead and instruct me through His Word as I studied. I was startled when reading Hebrews 11:33–34a, because the Holy Spirit put my name right at the beginning of verse 33. *"who through faith conquered kingdoms, administered justice, and gained what was promised; who shut the mouths of lions, quenched the fury of the flames, and escaped the edge of the sword; whose weakness was turned to strength; and who became powerful in battle . . ."* (NIV)

I knew this was God's battle, and I was only an instrument. *" . . . You won't [succeed] by might or by power, but by my Spirit, says the LORD of Armies."* (Zechariah 4:6b) The Lord further told me, *["But this kind does not go out except by prayer and fasting."]* (Matthew 17:21 NASB) I knew there were many walls to be broken down, and that only prayer with fasting could accomplish this. A word about fasting . . . to me it is simply denying self the pleasure of eating while having a humble attitude toward God and a heart full of praise.

Anointing is extremely beneficial in spiritual warfare. It is mentioned in both the Old and New Testaments, and is used for different reasons.

- The anointing was used to refresh the body. (II Chronicles 28:15)
- Purify the body. (Esther 2:12; Isaiah 57:9)
- Heal the sick. (Mark 6:13, James 5:14)
- Decorate a person. (Ruth 3:3)
- Prepare weapons for war. (Isaiah 21:5)
- Prepare the dead for burial. (Matthew 26:12, Mark 16:1, Luke 23:56)

The oil used in the anointing was applied to various parts of the body.

- The head. (Psalms 23:5, Ecclesiastes. 9:8)
- The face. (Psalms 104:15)
- The feet. (Luke 7:38–39, John 12:3)
- The eyes. (Revelation 3:18)

The oil or ointment that was used to anoint was expensive perfumed oil. This was one of the gifts brought to Jesus from the Wise Men.

To give myself wholly unto the Lord, each morning I would anoint my head, committing my thoughts to the Lord, my ears, that I might hear things in the way the Lord would desire, and my lips, asking God to give me the tongue of the learned. I would also anoint my hands and feet that the Lord would order my steps. Psalms 37:23 says, *"A person's steps are directed by the LORD, and the LORD delights in his way."*

- The anointing also guides into all truth. (I John 2:27)

- Consecrates us to God's service. (Exodus 30:29–32)
- Preserves those who receive. (Psalms 18:50, 20:6, 89:20–23)

Another benefit is that the anointing abides in the Christian believer. *"The anointing you received from Christ lives in you. You don't need anyone to teach you something else. Instead, Christ's anointing teaches you about everything. His anointing is true and contains no lie. So live in Christ as he taught you to do."* (I John 2:27)

Those who received the anointing were usually Kings, High Priests, and Prophets. The anointed were protected by God, and were not to be insulted, as they were God's servants with a calling. (I Samuel 24:6, 26:9) Because the anointing came from God, it was a sacred act, not to be imitated, or to be put on a stranger.

The anointing is a very powerful weapon in spiritual warfare. It provides a covering, strength, wisdom, and healings over our children, spouse, family, and friends, even our pets. However, this is not to be used carelessly! We should only anoint when we feel led by the Holy Spirit to do so. As we apply oil, we must do it in the Name of Jesus. The Name of Jesus holds the power in breaking the yoke. Of course, we need faith to believe in the power of the anointing. As mentioned earlier, the act of anointing is a sacred act and releases the power of the Holy Spirit to work in a situation as only He can. It does not matter if it is a baby's high fever, a child gone astray, a relationship, or a low or no balance in the checkbook . . . anoint that which needs God's help . . . in the Name of Jesus and BELIEVE.

God's Grace

During this time of adjustment, I diligently sought the Lord's help to overcome the challenges that were before me. I desired that His will would be done in this most critical situation. My reason for living was now gone, and the pain I felt sought to destroy my soul daily. I depended on the Lord for each breath I took, and in spite of my world falling apart, God's tender mercies and grace carried me. I seemed to be living above the circumstances, however, certainly not of my own power.

To this day, I cannot explain it, nor do I completely understand it. I believe that God just wanted me to accept His grace, which I gratefully did. It seemed that God placed me on a cloud to get through each day, until I could stand on my own again. My grief was soothed by the Holy Spirit through the *oil of joy* and the *garments (clothes) of praise*. Isaiah 61:3 proclaims, *"[He has sent me] to provide for all those who grieve in Zion, to give them crowns instead of ashes, the oil of joy instead of [tears of] grief, and clothes of praise instead of a spirit of weakness. They will be called Oaks of Righteousness, the Plantings of the LORD, so that he might display his glory."*

My length of time in this room was about one year.

Chapter Three - Room of Moving Mountains

A Different Realm

Shortly following the *Cloud of Grace*, I had a sense of being in another room. This room was distinctly a different realm than any I had ever experienced before. I truly had the sensation of separation from the people around me, although I talked with them every day. I am convinced this was a supernatural covering for carrying out this assignment, as I cannot begin to understand, nor explain it. The *Cloud of Grace* had lifted to a different degree, for now I was somewhat able to stand on my own two feet. God is so good! He carries us when we cannot handle the pressures of life. There was a definite presence between the outside world and myself that kept reality at bay. It kept the poison darts from penetrating my very being and affecting my faith.

The reason for calling this room "Moving Mountains" is due to the almost constant opposition we face from someone or something. This was not always related to the separation from my husband, for much of the time it was just the daily cares of life. However, the opposition always seemed bigger than I did. Looking back, I am sure that was the Lord's plan, causing me to stay 10,000% dependent on Him. God not only showed me how much I needed Him, but that I also needed to know what He could do, especially when in the natural the obstacles were insurmountable. The time in this room was extremely intense and lasted approximately three years.

More Fasting and Prayer

Each day was a new day in God's grace, but it was also another day where I had to face life. It seemed that around every corner there was another situation that drew me to the foot of the Cross. It may have only been a trying day on my part, but I was very dependent on Almighty God to get me through one hour at a time . . . let alone a day. During this hard and lonely period, I spent much time in fasting and prayer in order to build my faith. I fasted frequently for this reason, as during these times, our spirits are much more sensitive to the Holy Spirit.

Fasting has the following benefit–it strengthens both physically and spiritually.

- It will bring the blessings of obedience. (Matthew 6:14–18)
- Fasting brings humility through repentance. (Nehemiah 9:1–3)
- Many times, fasting gives the revelation of God's way for your future. (Daniel 9)
- It establishes authority and power for spiritual warfare. (Matthew 4:11)

Fasting is not a religious ritual. It is a privilege and blessing to approach God humbly, in wholehearted faith with your specific requests. Fasting is spiritual surgery. It can be compared to a doctor cutting away a physical problem to keep it from becoming larger, thereby restoring quality of life. Fasting focuses on attaining the mind of Christ, so that God can begin healing in the particular situation at hand. It was my responsibility to take care of myself in this manner. God instructs us to encourage ourselves in times of distress. If we allow circumstances to keep us down, what kind of warrior are we? Fasting was also necessary in seeking God for wisdom, when I was unable to find clear direction. It is evident in Isaiah Chapter 58 that fasting pleases God, telling us to fast when a situation calls for it. God deeply honors the faithfulness of His servants in this manner. I strongly encourage you to study the following Scriptures on fasting.

- I Samuel 1:7–20
- II Sam. 12:16–24
- II Chronicles 20:3,4
- Ezra 8:21
- Nehemiah 1:4–6
- Nehemiah 9:1,2
- Esther 4:16
- Job 33:19–26
- Jeremiah 14:12,13
- Matthew 17:21

There are many more examples of fasting in the Bible, as you will find when you continue your study.

NOTE: If you are on medication, or have potential physical limitations, please consult your physician before you initiate any fasting.

Standing on the Word

The Bible tells us sing psalms, hymns, and spiritual songs, and to have the mind of Christ. In order to be equipped for each day, my cup needed to be running over with the Word of God. One of the ways the Lord led me was to fill our home with the Word by playing Gospel music 24 hours a day. In explanation, I felt compelled to leave the music playing while at work, during the times of rest or sleep, or when just busy at home. This proved to be a gift of God's infinite wisdom. It filled our home with peace, regardless of what kind of day it was, and enabled me to seek God's wisdom when issues arose. The Holy Spirit would gently remind me each day of Psalms 46:10–11, *"Let go [of your concerns]! Then you will know that I am God. I rule the nations. I rule the earth. The LORD of Armies is with us. The God of Jacob is our stronghold. Selah"* Throughout the night, I would be absorbing the powerful and anointed Word of God as I slept. This restored my faith and strength at the end of each exhausting day. I knew my mind and my heart needed to be full of His Word. The more of God's promises I had engraved on my heart, the more my faith grew. This gave me more spiritual strength to come against the enemy in times of distressing news.

During this time of praying for my husband's soul and asking God to heal my marriage, I was led to submerge my husband's wedding ring in a bowl of olive oil. This would represent my marriage under the anointing! The anointing breaks the yokes of bondage that can cause traumas such as this in our lives. My husband's ring was covered with olive oil for three weeks, as this is how I felt the Lord leading. During this time, I spoke God's promises over this piece of my heart every day, at least once, but usually two or three times a day. I also declared that the anointing breaks the yoke in Jesus name, three or four times daily. Isaiah 10:27a, *"So it will be in that day, that his burden will be removed from your shoulders and his yoke from your neck, . . ."* (NASB) God tells us there is power in speaking His Word! In Genesis 1:3, *"Then God said, "Let there be light!" So there was light."* Our example is right there in the Holy Bible, to speak as God did. Approximately a year later, I was given instruction to repeat the anointing of my husband's ring. There were not any overnight miracles visible to the naked eye. Remember . . . according to Isaiah 55:11, God honors every act of faith as we declare His Word. *"My word, which comes from my mouth, is like the rain and snow. It will not come back to me without results. It will accomplish whatever I want and achieve whatever I send it to do."*

I believe God qualifies this through obedience. In other words, when we live according to His Word, keep our minds and hearts pure, and then we follow in the way He is leading us regarding our circumstances. Reflecting upon what our Lord has told us in Deuteronomy 28, it is quite clear that there are blessings for obedience and curses for disobedience. If we choose not to live according to the principles of God's Word, then He cannot fulfill His promises to us of the outpouring of His provision and blessing in our lives.

Jesus set the standard as our example in Matthew 27:46, when God the Father had to turn away from His only Son for a brief moment as Jesus bore all of humanity's sin on that cruel Cross. God cannot look upon sin, as He is Holy. Our Savior, the Lord Jesus Christ, was obedient, even unto death.

Allow me to explain and qualify this a little bit. The Lord had directed me in the beginning of this journey that this would be a most difficult and trying time. He also prepared my heart that this would require the utmost obedience and purity on my part in order for God to do the impossible in the heart of my beloved. This was due to the fact that this was a battle straight from the depths of hell to steal my husband's soul for eternity! Like an onion, there were layers upon layers of evil to break through and conquer before this battle would be won. In reference to scripture that was previously quoted, this is explained in Ephesians 6:11–13. *"Put on all the armor that God supplies. In this way you can take a stand against the devil's strategies. This is not a wrestling match against a human opponent. We are wrestling with rulers, authorities, the powers who govern this world of darkness, and spiritual forces that control evil in the heavenly world. For this reason, take up all the armor that God supplies. Then you will be able to take a stand during these evil days. Once you have overcome all obstacles, you will be able to stand your ground."*

Declaring God's Word became a daily practice and a way of life. Throughout the day, I would speak aloud His promises while driving to and from work.

I would also speak very quietly on the job, during break time, or when I had a moment alone. I knew there was power in speaking the Word! One of the many things God taught me during this period in my life was that the power of His Word is infallible, and it is one of the greatest privileges we have as children of the King. God tells us He puts His Word above His name in Psalms 138:2, *"I will bow toward your holy temple. I will give thanks to your name because of your mercy and truth. You have made your name and your promise greater than everything."* Understanding that every living thing came into existence through the very breath of God . . . putting His Word above His name speaks that His Word holds more power than we will ever need. For God to give His children the authority to use it is awesome! His Word is a weapon that will defeat the devil, our enemy, every time. One of the primary points of this writing is to make God's children aware of the mighty weapons we have available to fight our battles in life.

Just go before Almighty God, repent of your sins, and ask His guidance and strength in order to access these weapons. I share a psalm with you that is well worth repeating: *"A person's steps are directed by the LORD, and the LORD delights in his way. When he falls, he will not be thrown down headfirst because the LORD holds on to his hand."* (Psalms 37:23–24) Remember . . . be girded for battle, as explained in the Spiritual Warfare segment of Chapter 2. Because of our faith in speaking the Word, we are sustained by God's mercy and truth.

Remembering His Promises

Through my hours of prayer and reading of God's Word, there were too many Scriptures of instruction, hope, and promises to remember. I became frustrated when I could not remember a Word from the Lord I had read or heard 100 times, or so it seemed. Although perhaps sounding somewhat simple or insignificant, I realized that I needed God's help again. I felt directed to write them down. That proved to me one more time that I could not get through a day without the love, compassion, and patience of my Lord Jesus. I sat down with a handful of 3 x 5 index cards, along with some paper, and began writing down the promises, words of instruction, words of encouragement, and words of warning, one by one. From my experience of forgetting all the good God had in store for my family and me, I needed to stay focused, not forgetting all He had given me in His Word. I decided I would place these Scriptures on a common wall in the house. The bathroom wall and mirror is a common place, right? This way I would see them first thing in the morning, throughout the day and the last thing at night. I must say this was another marvelous idea from the Lord. As a result, I came to memorize most of them. Of the ones I could not fully memorize, I knew them well enough to quote the majority of the passages. This covered an area of about three feet by five feet. I had knocked the weapon of forgetfulness out of the enemy's hand. Thank you, Jesus!

Lack of Hope = Fear

I begin this segment with a prayer from Psalms 57:1–2, *"Have pity on me, O God. Have pity on me, because my soul takes refuge in you. I will take refuge in the shadow of your wings until destructive storms pass by. I call to God Most High, to the God who does everything for me."* Many women have experienced being left behind following a happy, secure marriage. This is not only extremely hurtful, but it can be very frightening. Resisting fear was one of my weakest areas - and the devil knew it. I was always fighting fear, which was why I needed to be full of God's Word. Not only does speaking the Word, and hearing the Word build faith, but it also dispels fear. I often came face to face with it. I believe my biggest fear at this time was never having my beloved all to myself again. I was not at the point of just walking away - we had too many priceless memories together. I could not forget them, and I would not lay them down, as they were a part of my inner being. After twenty years, I did not know how to live any other way.

In spite of committing myself to God anew every day, I had not mastered this part of it yet. This is what God wanted to accomplish in me . . . to depend on Him for my every need. At these low times, I had to encourage myself through prayer, singing, and speaking forth God's Word. I would go to the common wall in my home to pray and read every Scripture on the wall. This is what God had instructed, because my faith needed to be strong. This time with the Lord cleared my mind, rejuvenated my faith, and strengthened me overall. I was now in the proper frame of mind to receive what the Lord had for me through His Word. We are taught in God's Word that faith is what wins the victory. Romans 8:17–18 explains, *"If we are his children, we are also God's heirs. If we share in Christ's suffering in order to share his glory, we are heirs together with him. I consider our present sufferings insignificant compared to the glory that will soon be revealed to us."*

Power of the Tongue

As mentioned in a previous chapter, I knew I needed to change my thoughts and step up the faith, if I was going to fight for my husband's soul and my marriage. The Holy Spirit once again very bluntly gave me the following scripture for consideration. *"Your [own] mouth condemns you, not I. Your lips testify against you."* (Job 15:6) In other words, WATCH YOUR WORDS! There is power in the tongue! When you speak negatively, it will manifest as such. When you speak God's promises, He will perform miracles in your life.

More wisdom is found in Proverbs 18:21, *"The tongue has the power of life and death, and those who love to talk will have to eat their own words."* It is true; the words that spring forth from our lips can affect a situation. They can also change a person's actions for better . . . or worse . . . depending on what we say. By using the tongue rightly or wrongly, the fruit of it manifests itself, either good or bad. We do not realize the power our words hold. That is why God cautions us. To enforce this, I continued to write down every Scripture God gave me, whether it was encouragement, instruction, promise, or warning.

James 1:19–26, *"Remember this, my dear brothers and sisters: Everyone should be quick to listen, slow to speak, and should not get angry easily. An angry person doesn't do what God approves of. So get rid of all immoral behavior and all the wicked things you do. Humbly accept the word that God has placed in you. This word can save you. Do what God's word says. Don't merely listen to it, or you will fool yourselves. If someone listens to God's word but doesn't do what it says, he is like a person who looks at his face in a mirror, studies his features, goes away, and immediately forgets what he looks like. However, the person who continues to study God's perfect teachings that make people free and who remains committed to them will be blessed. People like that don't merely listen and forget; they actually do what God's teachings say. If a person thinks that he is religious but can't control his tongue, he is fooling himself. That person's religion is worthless."*

In the world we live in, there is much talk and teaching about the power of positive thinking. Some churches have their doctrine based on positive thinking. The Apostle Paul warns us in II Timothy 3:5, *"They will appear to have a godly life, but they will not let its power change them. Stay away from such people."* Yes, positive thinking has its place, but not as a religion as so many believe. Think about it . . . positive thinking does not have the power to heal or change a person's heart. Only our Sovereign God can perform such a work.

Instead of blaming God for our trials, let us open our ears and hearts to learn what God is endeavoring to teach us. If people would govern their tongues, they would save themselves much heartache and trouble. The worst thing we can bring to any dispute is anger. God is telling all humankind this principle . . . if only man would read God's Word and sit under the Word in a Bible teaching church. We must apply this to our daily living as well as our thought life. We must yield ourselves to the Word of God, with humble and teachable minds. We must also be willing to hear of our faults, humbly and graciously accepting reproof.

God Said, "Trust Me"

Although the following word of prophecy was given in October of 1994, I feel that God would have me share it with you at this time. It is not word for word, but reconstructed from my notes. *(Take comfort, I have anointed you for such a time as this. There are no coincidences. Everything that has happened I have ordered. I have put you in this place for a reason. Do not doubt My power, I can do greater things than you can imagine. For great things are upon you, says your Lord God)* WOW! This was a great encouragement to me. Again, words cannot express God's infinite wisdom, goodness, and compassion over our lives. There were several times throughout my lengthy journey I would ask for a word of confirmation that I was not holding to a wife's dream. I soon recognized this is a common trick of the devil, always trying to cause a believer to doubt God's infallible Word. I wrote this down and added it to my bathroom wall so I would see it every morning and every night.

If God has promised you physical healing, family restoration, or another type of miracle that only God can do, DO NOT GIVE UP AND DO NOT LET GO! If you are living a life pleasing to Him, God will answer! God answers in His infinite wisdom, and His timing is a part of His infinite wisdom. However, if we truly trust Him, we should then have the confidence that He is working all things for our good as stated in Romans 8:28–31, *"We know that all things work together for the good of those who love God— those whom he has called according to his plan. This is true because he already knew his people and had already appointed them to have the same form as the image of his Son. Therefore, his Son is the firstborn among many children. He also called those whom he had already appointed. He approved of those whom he had called, and he gave glory to those whom he had approved of. What can we say about all of this? If God is for us, who can be against us?"*

Here are more Scriptures that tell us why we can trust our God:

- Psalms 20:7
- Psalms 31:14,15
- Psalms 56:4
- Psalms 56:11
- Psalms 78:7
- Psalms 91:2–4

- Psalms 91:11–14
- Isaiah 12:2

There are times we have no other choice but to trust God . . . so why not give God a chance? What do you have to lose? It may be your only opportunity to regain your losses.

Waiting on God

I believe that our Lord God has the biggest waiting room in the universe. He often wills His saints to wait for a promise or an answer to prayer for many months, perhaps even years. Through my journey, I learned that waiting develops our faith. In time, we are able to believe for bigger and yet bigger things in God - for ourselves and for others. God also intends for us to share our experiences with others to encourage them in the only true faith. Life is full of challenges and unpleasant times. Challenges come as part of life with . . . or without God. I would much rather walk through life's dark valleys with God by my side. I know that many feel the need to escape the world's pressures through harmful substances such as drugs or alcohol. To the individuals who are ensnared by those pitfalls, I pray that you will take your needs, worries, and sorrows to Jesus. To prepare your heart, first ask Jesus to forgive your wrong thoughts and your wrong doings, replacing these sins with a pure heart. You are now ready to present your needs to our Lord and Savior. James tells us in Chapter 1, verses 2–4, *"My brothers and sisters, be very happy when you are tested in different ways. You know that such testing of your faith produces endurance. Endure until your testing is over. Then you will be mature and complete, and you won't need anything."*

I am aware that this is not easy medicine to swallow. However, when we meditate upon the sufferings that Jesus endured, it makes it more than acceptable. During times of study in the Word, I learned of many instances of saints waiting on God. Our Lord knows how impatient we can be, so He gave us plenty of examples of His servants in the days of old. Here are a few of them.

•	Hannah	I Samuel 1:2–5
•	David	Psalms 39:7–13
•	Isaiah	Isaiah 8:17
•	Micah	Micah 7:7,8
•	Joseph	Mark 15:43–46

Yes, God knows how difficult it is to wait. God also waits . . . He waits on men to get tired of playing games of pleasure the world has to offer - or people playing church. We have a tendency to be caught up in our own selfish motives and desires. We forget that we are dealing with a real heaven, a real hell, and a real God. *"Since we are surrounded by so many examples [of faith], we must get rid of everything that slows us down, especially sin that distracts us. We must run the race that lies ahead of us and never give up."* (Hebrews 12:1)

Do not quit! It never pays to give up simply because of impatience. Think carefully of what you are giving up and how it is going to affect your future, or your children's future. This is cause to stay in the Word, and not forsake church fellowship with those of like precious faith. Hebrews 10:24–26 makes it quite clear, *"We must also consider how to encourage each other to show love and to do good things. We should not stop gathering together with other believers, as some of you are doing. Instead, we must continue to encourage each other even more as we see the day of the Lord coming. If we go on sinning after we have learned the truth, no sacrifice can take away our sins."* God warns us not to be attracted to the ways of thinking that come from not being wise with our words or decisions. God will direct your path if you ask Him. However, God does not force His ways on anyone, He created us as free moral agents.

Hezekiah's Example

The Bible is full of examples for us to draw upon. I have come to love and appreciate God's Word so much because it is full of love and instruction on how to be joyous and content in a complex world. The story of Hezekiah really ministered to me during one of the most difficult times of my journey. As was mentioned before, this period was very intense. With all that was going on in my life, it was common sense to figure it was only a matter of time before my beloved would file for divorce. As Job said in Chapter 3, verse 25, *"What I feared has come upon me; what I dreaded has happened to me."* (NIV) When the time came to handle this most hurtful situation, I was not sure what I would do. No matter what I thought, whether it was the natural thought (which I was instructed by God not to do), or the supernatural, which was through God, there was no easy choice. After being cast aside for another woman, I felt useless, rejected, ugly, and as low as anyone can feel. I knew my husband did not love me or need me anymore. I did not know if I could continue this journey.

Who are we to say, "This is too hard!?" Through this experience, Jesus showed me how He did no wrong, but He was still rejected. Of course, my problem was nothing to compare with what my Lord Jesus suffered. Just the experience of one splinter of the Cross . . . spoke volumes of His love for humanity to me. Through His sufferings, He has saved everyone from Satan's grip. All we need to do is believe in Jesus, then accept and receive His salvation by faith. Jesus had the authority to call heaven's angels to remove Him from the suffering and pain of the Cross. He gave us the example to persevere! There was my answer . . . yes, Lord. I held tight to my Lord's hand and continued this unpleasant task set before me.

The story and example of Hezekiah is found in II Kings, Chapters 18 and 19. Hezekiah became king of Judah at the age of twenty-five. Hezekiah was a good and godly king. During his fourteenth year of reign, his entire kingdom was threatened by Sennacherib, the wicked king of Assyria. This threat came by way of a messenger. King Hezekiah was greatly disturbed by this, and he sent priests to the prophet Isaiah with a message about the threats. The prophet had words of encouragement from the Lord for Hezekiah. In II Kings 19:6–7 we read, *"Isaiah answered them, "Say this to your master, 'This is what the LORD says: Don't be afraid of the message that you heard when the Assyrian king's assistants slandered me. I'm going to put a spirit in him so that he will hear a rumor and return to his own country. I'll have him assassinated in his own country."* The prophet's answer was most uplifting, as it spoke of a speedy deliverance from the enemy. All the details . . . the blast, the rumor, the alarm that hastened Sennacherib's retreat, the destruction that overtook his army, and finally, the violent death that suddenly ended his career. God protects His people! This was a promise from God that king Hezekiah had not yet seen manifested, he had to believe it by faith. This is what God wants us to do today . . . live by faith and trust in Him.

I encourage you to read the rest of the story in II Kings Chapter 19 . . . it will bolster your faith. In verses 14–19, we learn that king Hezekiah received disturbing correspondence. *"Hezekiah took the letters from the messengers, read them, and went to the LORD's temple. He spread them out in front of the LORD and prayed to the LORD, "LORD of Armies, God of Israel, You are enthroned over the angels. You alone are God of all the kingdoms of the world. You made heaven and earth. Turn your ear toward me, LORD, and listen. Open your eyes, LORD, and see. Listen to the message that Sennacherib sent to defy the living God. It is true, LORD, that the kings of Assyria have leveled nations. They have thrown the gods from these countries into fires because these gods aren't real gods. They're only wooden and stone statues made by human hands. So the Assyrians have destroyed them. Now, LORD our God, rescue us from Assyria's control so that all the kingdoms on earth will know that you alone are the LORD God."*

Note this . . . Hezekiah did not waste any time, he went immediately to the temple. He laid the threats upon the altar, trusting God in faith to deliver him and his people. In verses 35–37, we are told, *"It happened that night. The LORD's angel went out and killed 185,000 [soldiers] in the Assyrian camp. When the Judeans got up early in the morning, they saw all the corpses. Then King Sennacherib of Assyria left. He went home to Nineveh and stayed there. While he was worshiping in the temple of his god Nisroch, Adrammelech and Sharezer assassinated him and escaped to the land of Ararat. His son Esarhaddon succeeded him as king."* The destruction was during the night; the officers and soldiers, secure in their might, were negligent, their discipline was relaxed, and the camp guards were not alert.

Here was my strength, encouragement, and instruction from God's Word. I took the papers from my husband to prayer the next morning, laying them upon the altar in my church. I then began my worship and praise before the Lord. At the point in my worship when I felt released to present my petitions, I proceeded to follow Hezekiah's example. Standing on the Word, I unequivocally believed then, as I do now, that I serve a God who does not change. He who parted the Red Sea, healed the blind, raised the dead, and destroyed 185,000 of Sennacherib's army to save Hezekiah's kingdom . . . this is the God I serve! I then left the church building and went to work that day trusting God would do a miracle. A couple of days later I felt led to hire an attorney to stop the proceedings of a potential divorce. This was also sending a message to my beloved that I loved him, and did not want a divorce. It was all in God's hands now, as we were not communicating at the time. I was again reminded of what the Lord had told me previously, *" . . . You won't succeed by might or by power, but by my Spirit, says the LORD of Armies."* (Zechariah 4:6b) I never heard or saw anything dealing with divorce ever again. Thank you Jesus!

A Common Trap

As was referred to earlier in this chapter, in Hebrews 10:25–26 we are admonished, *"We should not stop gathering together with other believers, as some of you are doing. Instead, we must continue to encourage each other even more as we see the day of the Lord coming. If we go on sinning after we have learned the truth, no sacrifice can take away our sins."*

In the midst of trials, it is normal to become weary and worn down. It is not my intent to sound repetitious, but the only way to remain above these circumstances is to stay full of His Word. Do not let the weight of the world cause you to be under the circumstances. Know in your heart that God will direct your steps to keep you from stumbling, as told to us in Psalms 37:23–24. This is another beautiful promise from God!

A classic ploy and tactic of our enemy is to cause us to be on the defensive with people. Unfortunately, many Christians become offended much too easily. Just remember, Christians are not perfect, just forgiven. It is easy to find an excuse to stay home. Beware of this trap, as the enemy has this snare out there for everyone! Once our emotions are stirred up, our natural human nature takes time to settle down, and some people take longer than others do. As a result, we do not want to go to church, which keeps us from feeding our spirits the awesome Word of God. This is the devil's plan to keep you out of church services, because that is where you become strong in the power and might of His Word.

Red Sea Experience

I call this my *Red Sea* experience, because I was running out of options, thoughts, and courage. This was one of the most difficult times in our separation. Because my husband and I looked at life and circumstances differently, we had many arguments. I must tell you that this was not normal in our relationship. For over twenty years, my beloved and I rarely had an argument. As I explained in the first chapter, we had a wonderful marriage.

Being full of anger, my husband had said some things that were very intimidating that frightened me. I was not used to these harsh, unkind words from my beloved. This was very disheartening . . . as these words were cold and unfeeling. These times would destroy me for days at a time. I felt the Lord was encouraging me to stop communication with him for a while, because of all the contention. There are times that the Lord requires us to handle some hard tasks. This was extremely difficult! This upset my husband, because I would not return his calls. I hated not answering his calls, or returning his messages. I was well aware that he did not understand, as he was not thinking with a clear mind at the time. It was hurting him, and I could not stand to hurt the man I loved. As I said, this was a horrible time in our separation, but I had to trust God and obey, as that was all I knew, because I didn't understand either . . .

Of course, I continued my praying, fasting, and reading His promises on my bathroom wall every day. It was the most difficult and most unbearable time in my life. There is no doubt in my mind that I could not have accomplished this assignment without the love and guidance of my Lord and Savior, Jesus Christ. God had allowed the cloud of grace to lift, causing me to face much of this with more natural emotions. Pressing into God became TOP PRIORITY, as the temptation to throw in the towel from the pain and anguish was overwhelming. However, the Bible promises us in I Corinthians 10:13 that He will allow no more than we can handle. *"There isn't any temptation that you have experienced which is unusual for humans. God, who faithfully keeps his promises, will not allow you to be tempted beyond your power to resist. But when you are tempted, he will also give you the ability to endure the temptation as your way of escape."*

The Crushed Rose Analogy

There were many challenges at this point, and each day gave yet another opportunity to trust God. I knew my Lord was Sovereign and in control, yet I could not help pleading, "Lord, why must this be so painful?" Shortly following one of these talks with God, I received a rhema (personal word) through the Holy Spirit that reflects the title of this book. I was given the analogy of a crushed rose. The deepest, compelling scent of a rose is concealed within its petals. The beautiful aroma cannot be enjoyed until the rose is smashed, bruised, or crushed. Before God is able to do certain works in our lives, we must have the ability to follow Him closely through His Word and His Spirit. In order for this to happen, we must go through a crushing process, an emptying out of our selfish desires and pride in order to allow room for godly attributes. It is difficult, painful, and even frightening; however, you will never be the same. Is it worth it? Yes! Keep in your mind and heart that it will only last for a season.

I realized that I needed to focus on the future, and once again lay my worries down, trusting in my Lord. There is much to be gained by trusting and following Him. Remember, God's battles may well involve someone's eternity. This is a very serious responsibility, as each of us must understand that we will answer to God for our actions . . . or inactions. When our Lord asks something of you, remember that life is but a vapor or mist, as explained in James 4:14. *"You don't know what will happen tomorrow. What is life? You are a mist that is seen for a moment and then disappears."* This is easy to see as we reflect upon the last days of Jesus. Although He was perfect and sinned not, He too had to be crushed in order that we might have eternal life.

Vision of Jesus' Embrace

Our Lord and Savior is such a personal God, He knows our every need before we ask. While driving home from work one day, the Lord gave me a vision. I truly do not recall when, or what transpired while driving, I just remember what Jesus showed me.

I was standing in my bedroom looking toward the hallway door. There, just inside the doorway, I saw Jesus embracing me. He held me to His bosom with His gentle arms securely wrapped around me . . . just as a loving mother would hold her frightened or hurting child. He was and still is my refuge, my shelter, my strength, and my life. I could hardly contain myself that He would give His sacred head for such a worm as I.

The Lord of lords and King of kings gave to me a priceless gift that would affect me for the rest of my days. Everything I had been striving for came to life with a new meaning. Jesus truly had been with me the whole time! The reality of Jesus' awesome love renewed and refreshed my spirit! He really does love me . . . enough to die for me, just as we are told in John 3:16–17. *"For God so loved the world that he gave his one and only Son, that whoever believes in him shall not perish but have eternal life. For God did not send his Son into the world to condemn the*

world, but to save the world through him." (NIV)
This vision gave me the additional strength I needed
for the duration of this journey. The revelation of
how Jesus patiently waits for us, along with the deep
love He has for all of us, brought indescribable joy
to my soul. Never doubt His love, even if you do not
feel it at times! On the authority of His Word, the
Holy Bible, I guarantee you that He is there!

Shadow of the Cross

In April of 1994, while attending a Ladies
Retreat, I received another word of encouragement
from my Lord; *"There are great things ahead, wait
for them."* I would experience moments such as this
to gird me for an upcoming difficult day or week. I
would frequently reflect on these words from God.
Following this much needed retreat, I returned home
only to find a letter in my mailbox saying I must
move. The homeowner wanted to sell the home I was
living in. I was distraught. In most cases, it would not
be a problem, just move, right? Unfortunately, not so
easy in this case. Remember, the Lord had instructed
me not to communicate with my husband at this
time. Understandably, no communication between
us upset him, so therefore he was unwilling to help. I
was also on limited income, and truly was unsure of
what to do. It's me again, Lord!

As a few weeks passed, it became evident that
I had to move. I did ask the Lord to intervene, so that
I might be able to remain in my home. At this time,
God had other plans for me. This was a time of great
uncertainty. I resolved to continue following God

and trust in His Word. *"My thoughts are not your thoughts, and my ways are not your ways,"* declares the LORD." Isaiah 55:8

My friend of many years graciously opened her home to me. I was blessed as my God, Jehovah-Jireh (The Lord Will Provide), continued to provide for my every need, regardless how small or how large. The size of a need does not matter to God. He is also El Shaddai (God Almighty or The All-Sufficient and All-Bountiful One). I made preparations to move. On moving day, my friend and I were working on our final load before turning off the lights and closing the door for the last time. It was about midnight, and we were taking one final look when a large shadow of a cross appeared on the south wall of the garage. This cross seemed to be 6–7 feet tall and stretched across approximately 5–6 feet wide, and outlined with lace. I thought for sure I was overtired and seeing things, so in my mind I diligently tried to explain this large shadow away. I could not, so I asked my friend to look at the garage wall to see if she saw anything. She saw it immediately! We both checked outside and around the property to find what might be casting that shadow. We looked for almost 10 minutes, but found nothing that could cause it! It was obvious to both of us that this was a supernatural sign from the Lord God. We both recognized it as confirmation from Him that everything was in His hands and we were doing the right thing. God is so good!

This is the Day that the Lord Hath Made
The move was now complete. Peace resided in

all of us that this was God's plan for the moment. Although life was calm for a time, I had to came to the realization that if it was not for my friend and her family, I could have been looking at staying in a shelter. I could not think about that . . . God had provided and that is where my thoughts needed to stay. God instilled in my heart the following passages in Matthew 6:25–27, *"So I tell you to stop worrying about what you will eat, drink, or wear. Isn't life more than food and the body more than clothes? Look at the birds. They don't plant, harvest, or gather the harvest into barns. Yet, your heavenly Father feeds them. Aren't you worth more than they? Can any of you add a single hour to your life by worrying?"* The Lord had to remind me I was a child of El Shaddai, God Almighty. This was a commandment from the Lord: be not concerned about the daily cares of food, shelter, or income, because He would provide. This is easier said than done . . . However, the Lord was right, what does worrying solve?

As always, the Lord had instructed me to live each day with my eyes on Him, not on the circumstances. I went forth in peace and joy, declaring the victory in Jesus name! In spite of the peace that was in my heart, this was very difficult and sad time.

Nevertheless, God had taught me that He would not only honor my obedience in waiting, but He would strengthen me so that I would not grow weary. Isaiah 40:31 uplifted me, *"Yet, the strength of those who wait with hope in the LORD will be renewed. They will soar on wings like eagles. They will run and won't become weary. They will walk and won't grow tired."* My sweet and loving Lord Jesus assured me that He would restore everything–and more–that the enemy had stolen from me. *"I will repay you for the years the locusts have eaten—the great locust and the young locust, the other locusts and the locust swarm, . . .* (Joel 2:25a, NIV)

All I needed to do now was wait upon the LORD . . .

Chapter Four - Room of Encouragement

The Grace and Tender Mercies of God

Looking back over the past three years, I had clearly seen the hand of God in His infinite wisdom, bountiful grace, and bounds of mercy. There was no way I could have walked through this valley without my Lord and Savior. The Lord promised me in Isaiah 41:18, *"I will make rivers flow on bare hilltops. I will make springs flow through valleys. I will turn deserts into lakes. I will turn dry land into springs."* He also gave me Isaiah 43:1–2 as another beautiful promise, *"The LORD created Jacob and formed Israel. Now, this is what the LORD says: Do not be afraid, because I have reclaimed you. I have called you by name; you are mine. When you go through the sea, I am with you. When you go through rivers, they will not sweep you away. When you walk through fire, you will not be burned, and the flames will not harm you."* He would be with me through it all.

I depended on a fresh vial of God's mercy each morning, *"It is new every morning. His faithfulness is great. My soul can say, 'The LORD is my lot [in life]. That is why I find hope in him.' The LORD is good to those who wait for him, to anyone who seeks help from him. It is good to continue to hope and wait silently for the LORD to save us."* (Lamentations 3:23–26) It was only by God's grace that I made it to the end of the day in one piece. I remember reading in Matthew when Jesus went to the Garden of Gethsemane to pray. That is where He found the strength and grace to continue His journey of grief, pain, and heartache. Jesus knew the road ahead was treacherous. I am sure He wept daily to His Father in heaven. I know my Jesus, and although He was agonizing over His pain and heartache to come, Jesus wept for the people, and He prayed for each one of them. Even more difficult, He forgave them and then asked His Father to forgive them. Jesus no doubt prayed and wept for Judas, the disciple who betrayed Him. This is having a clean heart and clean hands, wishing no harm to anyone in spite of their devious and unkind acts toward you. Praying for the one who has hurt you is necessary and part of the healing process. Remember, God cannot work where there is iniquity, in other words, sin or wickedness, anywhere in your life. In my time with the Lord, I found the grace through prayer to forgive my husband and the "other woman." We are told in Mark 11:25, *"Whenever you pray, forgive anything you have against anyone. Then your Father in heaven will forgive your failures."*

Around this time, the Lord led me into another room. This room was quite different, distinctly refreshing. As I journeyed through this room, I received many encouragements from my Lord. He showed me repeatedly that He was leading me toward the end of this chapter in my life.

A New Season
Times remained difficult, yet the Lord saw fit

to send encouragement my way. This was a time of new and refreshing hope following a very long season of challenges. It seemed everywhere I looked or went I would receive a confirmation of my beloved coming home. For example, I was in a store and a song about the reunion of a husband and wife started playing. Another time, on the way to work I saw a billboard that had "don't quit" printed on it. Many times, someone's personal license plate encouraged me; it specifically said "LAF." This message was put in front of me several times a week. I knew in my spirit that this was instruction to laugh, in the midst of moments that were particularly difficult.

I also received tremendous encouragement while sitting under the Word of God in my church. I continued to stand on His Word according to Hebrews 10:23, *"We must continue to hold firmly to our declaration of faith. The one who made the promise is faithful."* I also responded to altar calls as I felt the Lord leading. In a service in October of 1994, I received a prophetic word through my Pastor while at the altar. While he was praying over me, he suddenly stopped and said; "Shelley, something just broke." To me this meant the time was coming closer when I would embrace my wonderful husband again. How encouraging, what a moment of rejuvenation and strength to my weak and tired spirit. This proved to build up my faith and prayer life. I now prayed with a new fervency, a new hope, and new joy! *"His anger lasts only a moment. His favor lasts a lifetime. Weeping may last for the night, but there is a song of joy in the morning."* (Psalms 30:5)

My beloved was on his way home! This journey was soon going to be part of my past. One of the many promises I spoke and declared every day was previously mentioned, but it bears repeating, as it was profound in my life. This is the promise spoken in Joel 2:25–27, *"I will repay you for the years the locusts have eaten—the great locust and the young locust, the other locusts and the locust swarm—my great army that I sent among you. You will have plenty to eat, until you are full, and you will praise the name of the LORD your God, who has worked wonders for you; never again will my people be shamed. Then you will know that I am in Israel, that I am the LORD your God, and that there is no other; never again will my people be shamed."* (NIV)

The Power of Praise

Sometime later, while working in my room at my friend's home, I saw a shadow on the bedroom wall that resembled a huge man lying on his back face up, as if he was sleeping. Looking around, I saw nothing in the room that could cast a shadow of that nature and shape. I called out to my friend who was in an adjoining room, for a second opinion. I explained the shadow to her, which was still there, and she agreed that it looked like a large man sleeping. We were unsure what to think, except that this was very strange and different.

Just a few hours later, at approximately 1 a.m., my friend came in and woke me up rather excitedly. She had just awakened from a dream about this shadow. The Lord explained to her in this dream that the shadow was my husband trapped in chains, barely able to move. He was trapped and in bondage by the enemy! This was confirmation of what I felt in my spirit near the beginning of this journey. The Lord also showed my friend that my husband was beginning to move, or wake up, as these chains were breaking . . . from the constant warfare of fasting, worship, and prayer! I immediately thought that perhaps this was what my Pastor received when he told me "Something just broke."

It was during this same period that the Lord led my friend and I, and our two children into a late night prayer meeting. After a normal evening, as we were all saying our goodnights to each other, my friend felt the Lord leading the four of us to hold hands and enter into His presence in worship. This was a one-of-a-kind prayer meeting, and we unquestionably obeyed the Lord's leading. There were no breaks, no visiting the bathroom, no talking to one another . . . only worship and praise. This time spent in the presence of the Lord lasted two solid hours. Before the Lord led to close this prayer meeting, He gave my friend a word in response to this act of obedience; *"I have heard you my children, My work is done."* The Lord was there in our midst. For it was only by His presence that we had the strength and the discipline to accomplish this work. During the hour or so following, the four of us sat around the living room and tried to figure out what just transpired. What did it mean? The Holy Spirit prompted me to remember Apostle Paul's explanation in II Corinthians 10:3–5, *"Of course we are human, but we don't fight like humans. The weapons we use in our fight are not made by humans. Rather, they are powerful weapons from God. With them we destroy people's defenses, that is, their arguments and all their intellectual arrogance that oppose the knowledge of God. We take every thought captive so that it is obedient to Christ."*

This was obviously a crucial night in the spirit. After sharing our thoughts with one another, we equated this night to our personal *Passover*. This was in the sense that when the blood was placed on the doorposts of the Israelites of the Old Testament, the death angel could not touch that particular household. It had to pass by, because of the covering and power of the blood. Our praise and worship gave God what was needed to break the hold Satan had on my beloved through deception and lies. A supernatural act occurred that night, a miracle that only God Almighty could do through the power of worship and praise!

I am sure that you will notice that this chapter is much shorter than the previous ones. This is very simply due to the fact that my long journey was coming to a close, although I still had one more 'room' to go, so to speak. The length of time spent in this room was approximately five to six months.

Before entering the next room, I leave you with the following verses from I John 5:3–5, *"To love God means that we obey his commandments. Obeying his commandments isn't difficult because everyone who has been born from God has won the victory over the world. Our faith is what wins the victory over the world. Who wins the victory over the world? Isn't it the person who believes that Jesus is the Son of God?"* AMEN.

Communing with God

"Indeed, the time is coming, and it is now here, when the true worshipers will worship the Father in spirit and truth. The Father is looking for people like that to worship him. God is a spirit. Those who worship him must worship in spirit and truth." (John 4:23–24)

Acceptable worship is based upon faith and obedience. In Genesis 22:3, Abraham responded without hesitating, even though God commanded that he sacrifice his own son. What faith! Abraham understood worship to mean the costliest sacrifice he had ever been called on to make. Yet he had no malice in his heart, he was willing to sacrifice his son in humble obedience. I cannot begin to conceive that thought! True worship requires a complete renunciation of self, meaning that God and His will comes before our own will and desires. We learn that obedience is a part of and essential to true worship. Worship is not used for self-expression, but rather submission of self in spirit and truth to the will of God. The true worshipper is one who worships God in the spirit, rejoices in Christ Jesus, and has no confidence in worldly things. (See Philippians 3:2–3)

A person can be involved in the exercise of acts of worship to God. However, with the wrong condition of heart, they can be eternally lost. We read in

Amos 5:20–27, how God responds to worship that is not given with a clean and pure heart. *"The day of the LORD brings darkness and not light. It is pitch black, with no light. I hate your festivals; I despise them. I'm not pleased with your religious assemblies. Even though you bring me burnt offerings and grain offerings, I won't accept them. I won't even look at the fellowship offerings of your choicest animals. Spare me the sound of your songs. I won't listen to the music of your harps. But let justice flow like a river and righteousness like an ever-flowing stream. Did you bring me sacrifices and grain offerings in the desert for 40 years, nation of Israel? You carried along the statues of [the god] Sikkuth as your king and the star Kiyyun, the gods you made for yourselves. I will send you into exile beyond Damascus, says the LORD, whose name is the God of Armies."*

Worship is to do just what God desires, nothing more, nothing less. Worship in spirit must come from a humble, forgiving heart, as we give God praise, honor, and glory by recognizing His place of absolute supremacy in all things. We find in Psalms 89:7–8, *"In the council of the holy ones God is greatly feared; he is more awesome than all who surround him. O LORD God Almighty, who is like you? You are mighty, O LORD, and your faithfulness surrounds you."* (NIV)

When we read in Isaiah Chapter 53 how Jesus was bruised, crushed, and pierced for us, how can we deny our Lord true worship and praise? His love and forgiveness only grew stronger, in spite of the inhumane treatment He received. If you do not know His goodness, or know Him as a friend, I encourage you to believe on Him as your Savior. His sufferings and death through the Crucifixion bought your ticket to heaven! All you need to do is accept His Atonement with a repentant and humble heart.

Each morning before entering the sanctuary, I would prepare my heart. This enabled me to enter immediately into worship with a clean heart and clean hands as we read about in Psalms 24:4–5, *"He who has clean hands and a pure heart, who does not lift up his soul to an idol or swear by what is false. He will receive blessing from the LORD and vindication from God his Savior."* (NIV) Another wonderful passage is found in Psalms 86:8, *"Among the gods there is none like you, O Lord; no deeds can compare with yours."* (NIV) Lifting His name on high and declaring His holiness, the Lord and I began to commune.

This precious time the Lord and I spent together produced a bond of love and trust that transformed my life. I never dreamed that I would be honored to come to know our Lord and Savior Jesus Christ as a true friend and confidant. As I prayed, His presence was so real; I could sense myself standing before Him offering sacrificial praise and worship. There was a sense of protection from all the evil in the world, not to mention the peace the Lord imparted to me through our time together. When this part of my day ended, I left strong, encouraged, and secure in the Lord. Nothing can ever replace these times with the Lord. Once you taste of God's presence, you will not settle for anything less, I assure you that you will hunger and thirst for more. His presence restores, encourages, and rebuilds. *"Taste and see that the LORD is good; blessed is the man who takes refuge in him."* (Psalms 34:8, NIV)

God promised in Hebrews 11:6 that He rewards those who diligently seek Him.

In worship, approach God with a clean and repentant heart. In faith, believe in His Word, and then expect answers to your prayers. I share Luke 6:38 with you, *"Give, and you will receive. A large quantity, pressed together, shaken down, and running over will be put into your pocket. The standards you use for others will be applied to you."* Without having faith in God to answer our prayers, it is impossible to please Him. It pleases God to know His people are exercising faith and trusting Him to answer our prayers. Worship will always produce great joy in the heart of the worshipper.

I must warn you that once you make a commitment to worship and prayer, putting your trust in the Lord, you will find that opposition and distraction will come your way. This will come straight from our adversary, the devil, as he and his minions will delight in working to keep you from fulfilling your commitment. It is not my intention to give him any credit for anything, but the devil is excellent at his job. Anything he can do to cause stress, confusion, or complication in your life, he will.

Living by Faith

By this time, the Lord had taught me the value of trusting in Him. We are told in Proverbs 3:5–6,

"Trust the LORD with all your heart, and do not rely on your own understanding. In all your ways acknowledge him, and he will make your paths smooth. " According to this promise from God, we are to trust Him, and He will direct our steps and paths. The Hebrew word for trust is "batach." It means to have confidence, or to feel secure with no fear whatsoever. To me, that meant to cast all my fears away, having complete and total trust in my Lord Jesus. Lasting trust is based on how much we really know and depend upon our Lord and Savior. We come to know Him the same way we make a new friend, by spending time with Him. This is accomplished by reading the Word, and spending quality time in worship and prayer.

Again, I refer to Hebrews 10:23, where we learn of faith; *"We must continue to hold firmly to our declaration of faith. The one who made the promise is faithful. "* Consider these three examples of people who trusted God with all their hearts, even in difficult times:

- Job–*"If God would kill me, I would have no hope [left]. Nevertheless, I will defend my behavior to his face. This also will be my salvation because no godless person could face him. "* (Job 13:15–16) Note Job's statement of trust in Job 42:1–6. *"Then Job answered the LORD, "I know that you can do everything and that your plans are unstoppable. [You said,] 'Who is this that belittles my advice without having any knowledge [about it]?' Yes, I have* stated things I didn't understand, things too mysterious for me to know. [You said,] 'Listen now, and I will speak. I will ask you, and you will teach me.' I had heard about you with my own ears, but now I have seen you with my own eyes. That is why I take back what I said, and I sit in dust and ashes to show that I am sorry."

- Habakkuk–"Even if the fig tree does not bloom and the vines have no grapes, even if the olive tree fails to produce and the fields yield no food, even if the sheep pen is empty and the stalls have no cattle—even then, I will be happy with the LORD. I will truly find joy in God, who saves me. The LORD Almighty is my strength. He makes my feet like those of a deer. He makes me walk on the mountains . . ." (Habakkuk 3:17–19a)

- Jesus Christ–Jesus prayed about the matter, and so should we. We read in Matthew 26:36–46, "Then Jesus went with his disciples to a place called Gethsemane, and he said to them, "Sit here while I go over there and pray." He took Peter and the two sons of Zebedee along with him, and he began to be sorrowful and troubled. Then he said to them, "My soul is overwhelmed with sorrow to the point of death. Stay here and keep watch with me." Going a little farther, he fell with his face to the ground and prayed, "My Father, if it is possible, may this cup be taken from me. Yet not as I will, but as you will." Then he returned to his disciples and found them sleeping. "Could you men not

keep watch with me for one hour?" he asked Peter. "Watch and pray so that you will not fall into temptation. The spirit is willing, but the body is weak." He went away a second time and prayed, "My Father, if it is not possible for this cup to be taken away unless I drink it, may your will be done." When he came back, he again found them sleeping, because their eyes were heavy. So he left them and went away once more and prayed the third time, saying the same thing. Then he returned to the disciples and said to them, "Are you still sleeping and resting? Look, the hour is near, and the Son of Man is betrayed into the hands of sinners. Rise, let us go! Here comes my betrayer!"
(NIV)

Why do we need God's direction? It is because daily life is difficult and filled with many pitfalls. There are dangers we do not always recognize or perceive. We are fallible and many times do not know what to do. The following is a beautiful piece of God's Word from the Psalms that is full of promises for you and I. *"Nun. Your word is a lamp to my feet and a light for my path. I have taken an oath and confirmed it, that I will follow your righteous laws. I have suffered much; preserve my life, O LORD, according to your word. Accept, O LORD, the willing praise of my mouth, and teach me your laws. Though I constantly take my life in my hands, I will not forget your law. The wicked have set a snare for me, but I have not strayed from your precepts. Your statutes are my heritage forever; they are the joy of my heart. My heart is set on keeping your decrees to the very end. Samekh. I hate double-minded men, but I love your law. You are my refuge and my shield; I have put my hope in your word. Away from me, you evildoers, that I may keep the commands of my God! Sustain me according to your promise, and I will live; do not let my hopes be dashed. Uphold me, and I will be delivered; I will always have regard for your decrees."* (Psalms 119:105–117, NIV)

Read this every day and trust God to perform His work in your life. The Apostle Paul tells us in Philippians 4:6–7, *"Never worry about anything. But in every situation let God know what you need in prayers and requests while giving thanks. Then God's peace, which goes beyond anything we can imagine, will guard your thoughts and emotions through Christ Jesus."*

The example Jesus left for us shows us the direction our lives should take. *"God called you to endure suffering because Christ suffered for you. He left you an example so that you could follow in his footsteps."* (I Peter 2:21) Although we can never completely comprehend God's ways, we must trust His ways. The following passage from Isaiah was mentioned earlier, however, I repeat it because it speaks volumes. *"My thoughts are not your thoughts, and my ways are not your ways,"* declares the LORD. *"Just as the heavens are higher than the earth, so my ways are higher than your ways, and my thoughts are higher than your thoughts."* (Isaiah 55:8–9)

Trusting God with the priceless jewels of

your life is no easy task. My experience took almost four years before I totally rested in God's Word and trusted that He was working all things for my good. Romans 8:28 promises us, *"We know that all things work together for the good of those who love God— those whom he has called according to his plan."* I practiced trusting Him every day, by reading His Word and earnestly praying. As I stated earlier, this was the only place I could find peace and rest from the heart wrenching circumstances. This caused me to keep returning to His Word, emptying the depths of my soul at His feet.

I spent about four to five months in this room. However, the principles I have shared with you are eternal. The practice of worship and prayer is an ongoing part of my earthly life that will continue until I see Jesus in Heaven. In that day, I will have the awesome privilege of worshiping my Lord for all eternity, along with all of the believers who have gone before.

Chapter Six - Room of Prophecies

A Living Sacrifice

Walking this weary road had established the desire within my whole being to love, serve and worship my Jesus. I awoke each morning realizing I was alive due to His tender mercies and love. I knew in my spirit then as well as now, that there is never a better time to worship the Lord than the present. According to the Holy Bible, we are called to be living sacrifices. What a privilege . . . a calling to commune one-on-one with Almighty God! Think about it . . . the Creator of all humanity and the universe wants to be your best friend! I mentioned this before, but talking with God is like talking to your favorite sister or brother. One who does not criticize you, but one who helps you. To have Jesus as a best friend is a gift available only to those who call Him Lord. We can tell Him our deepest fears and they will not go any further! He will embrace you in the middle of the night when you cannot sleep. He can heal your aching heart and soothe your mixed and torn emotions. He is a friend who is there for you, while everyone else is running the race of life. Offering yourself as a living sacrifice provides a refuge from the world. *"Brothers and sisters, in view of all we have just shared about God's compassion, I encourage you to offer your bodies as living sacrifices, dedicated to God and pleasing to him. This kind of worship is appropriate for you. Don't become like the people of this world. Instead, change the way you think. Then you will always be able to determine what God really wants—what is good, pleasing, and perfect."* (Romans 12:1–2)

Prophecies

The Merriam-Webster dictionary defines prophecy with three different meanings:

- The function of a prophet, an utterance under an inspiring influence of a religious experience,
- divinely inspired moral teaching, as by warning, exhorting or consoling,
- a declaration of something to come; a prediction.

In this "Room of Prophecies," I received many exhortations from God. I feel led to share some of these most personal experiences between my Lord and me. I trust and pray that they will be an encouragement, building your faith and hope. These very words kept my faith focused on God and His Word. He does not mislead or misrepresent His Word. God Almighty has made it clear in His Word that He goes before us as He says in Isaiah 45:2, *"I will go before you and will level the mountains; I will break down gates of bronze and cut through bars of iron."* (NIV) A true believer of Jehovah God never walks alone. (NOTE: The prophecies that are not in quotes are paraphrased from my notes.)

One of the first prophecies that indicated my journey was nearing the end came to me in the latter part of 1994. An exhortation came forth stating, *"Look behind you, I carried you . . ."* There was more, but this was what caught my attention. The prophecy went on to say look what He has brought me through up to this point. When I heard this spoken to the church body, I sensed warmth in my spirit, an indication to me this was a word from the Lord to me. It was difficult for me to accept personally, as I was still in the midst of the storm, feeling no relief. This is because nothing had changed in the natural, but I knew that this message was to be received on a spiritual level. By February of 1995, two more prophecies came forth.

- February 4, 1995 - *The past is past, I have led you through a multitude of problems. I have been and am in control of the past, the present, and the future. I have taken you through these trials to bring you to this place in me. You would have not made it through without me. All of your enemies will remain under your feet as long as you remember who your source is.*
- February 23, 1995 - *Daughter, thy faith has made thee whole. Go in peace to your promised land.*

As you can see by the time lapse here, God does not live by a calendar. I learned that when God spoke in the present tense it would not manifest in the natural for a few weeks, perhaps even months. The key was to hold on to God's promise and not waiver in my faith. Nevertheless, it was food for my spirit to remain focused on the eternal value of these precious words from my Lord, rather than my daily struggles.

Wells of Baca

A *word of knowledge* is not the same as a *word of prophecy*. A *word of knowledge* is the oracle (divinely inspired message) of God spoken from one of God's faithful servants. While attending a women's retreat, I received a *word of knowledge* from one such faithful servant saying that the *wells of Baca* had been established. This woman further explained to me that I had made wells in this valley for others to drink from as they were in their valley. I confess that at the time I was not familiar with the *wells of Baca*. I found reference to this in Psalms 84:6, *"Who passing through the valley of Baca make it a well; the rain also filleth the pools."* (KJV)

In some translations, the Valley of Baca is called the Valley of Weeping. The root word *baca* means weeping. The trees or shrubs depicted here were known as *weepers*. This was due to the way that tree sap or moisture leaked from them. Spiritually, the Valley of Baca (Weeping) is an analogy or expression of the experiences of those whose faith and strength is in God. They find that through His grace their sorrows have turned into blessings.

In coming to a spiritual understanding of this message from God, I realized that I was leading the way for others who would follow. I knew that the fiery trials I walked through would leave a mark on many hearts. Some of these marks would be ones of encouragement in times of sorrow, while others would be of courage in the times of fear and pain. This gave me more insight into how the Lord would use this period in my life for others. The prayer of my heart is that you, the reader, would experience our Sovereign God in an unforgettable way. I pray that the Holy Spirit will remove all preconceived notions and doubts you may have toward your Creator, Whom before you will one day stand.

More Prophecies

- June 18, 1995 - *I have told you things would come against you and not to fear them–for you have overcome the world through me. These trials are to strengthen you. No weapon formed against you shall prosper.* (see Isaiah 54:17) *All things work together for good for those who love me and keep me first in their lives.* (see Romans 8:28)

- June 25, 1995 - *"Don't be discouraged, I will draw close to you."* There was more to this message. However, these words sent a chill through me, as I was reminded that I was not walking the road alone . . .

Joy Comes In The Morning

Psalms 30:5 tells us, *"His anger lasts only a moment. His favor lasts a lifetime. Weeping may last for the night, but there is a song of joy in the morn-*

ing. " What a beautiful promise for the faithful! In Psalms 40:3 we read, *"He placed a new song in my mouth, a song of praise to our God. Many will see this and worship. They will trust the LORD. "*

In the month of September 1995, I received another prophecy: *I am with you this morning, I have seen the effort you have put forth to be here. I have seen your faith and have honored it. I have brought you through the valley of the shadow of death. I have not led you astray. If you will endure to the end, you will have a glorious land. Do not follow man, I will lead you.* The Lord was specific from the very beginning of my journey . . . keep my eyes and my heart focused on Him. Paul teaches us in I Corinthians 2:14, *"A person who isn't spiritual doesn't accept the teachings of God's Spirit. He thinks they're nonsense. He can't understand them because a person must be spiritual to evaluate them. "* I admit that did not understand much of what God had instructed me during this time. However, I knew I was not to question Almighty God, so I prayed for grace and obeyed. *"So, then, brothers and sisters, don't let anyone move you off the foundation [of your faith]. Always excel in the work you do for the Lord. You know that the hard work you do for the Lord is not pointless. "* (I Corinthians 15:58) This prophecy was full of hope and victory–for the Lord had given me instruction, encouragement, and a promise.

Yet another prophecy . . .

- November 1995 - *I am taking you through these difficult times not to cause failure, but to teach you to lean on me.*

This was additional insight on why this journey was part of God's plan for my life. Our omnipotent God knows all things. He knew what I needed to reach that place in Jesus. There is only one place we can find peace, hope, strength, love, and acceptance in times of darkness . . . that place is in Jesus!

Times remained difficult, and I knew what God had said and promised, but I was extremely weary. My precious Lord gave me Isaiah 32:16–17 on a particularly trying day, *"Then justice will live in the wilderness, and righteousness will be at home in the fertile field. Then an act of righteousness will bring about peace, calm, and safety forever."* God is so good! What a personal God we serve . . . I love my Jesus!

The Whirlwind

One morning in December of 1995, my friend had experienced a mighty move of the Holy Spirit, which she described as a whirlwind. The experience was so powerful she was overwhelmed and could not contain her tears. This left the impression as though something great had been accomplished or broken in the spirit. Referring to the prophecy spoken by God in September . . . He has seen my faith and honored it. God speaks of a whirlwind in Proverbs 10:25, *"When the whirlwind passes, the wicked is no more, But the righteous has an everlasting foundation."* (NASB) On January 6, 1996, there was a distinct cloud formation showing a whirlwind in the sky! We serve an awesome and loving God!

The Time is Near

It had been approximately a year and a half since my friend invited me stay with her and her family. I experienced an excitement in my spirit, because about this time God began to speak to my heart about moving into my own apartment. I knew the reason for this was that my beloved would be coming home soon. As the Lord continued to prepare my heart for my husband's homecoming, He gave me the instruction written to wives in I Peter 3:4, *"Rather, beauty is something internal that can't be destroyed. Beauty expresses itself in a gentle and quiet attitude which God considers precious."* The Lord was telling me to keep my mouth closed and hugs readily available. This was not contingent on how I felt, how my day was going, or what the circumstances were. We should never take God's instruction lightly. I knew this was crucial, for my beloved had been out in the world for many years with the wolves. John 10:12 describes the wolf as one who destroys and devours. He would come home physically and mentally drained, wounded, and broken from the world. With this and much more on my heart, I knew I must watch my words, just as the Lord instructed. I did not have the luxury to sit on the pity pot, or take offense . . . not if I wanted God to use me to restore my marriage. My husband had made mistakes, but he was still the man God had given me to have and to hold until death do us part. I loved him very much and wanted to be instrumental in his restoration.

"However, as it is written: "No eye has seen, no ear has heard, no mind has conceived what God has prepared for those who love him"—but God has revealed it to us by his Spirit. The Spirit searches all things, even the deep things of God." (I Corinthians 2:9–10 NIV) Once again, God's promise kept me focused. I desired nothing more than what I had been diligently seeking for the last five years . . .

The Spoken Word

Going back to December 1995, God had given another specific instruction. This time it was for our 15-year-old son, Jason. He was to read a certain passage aloud in his Dad's house that weekend. This was because when we speak God's word *aloud* it overpowers the works of the enemy. This action breaks the yoke of bondage for loved ones. Isaiah tells us in Chapter 10, verse 27, *"And it shall come to pass in that day, that his burden shall be taken away from off thy shoulder, and his yoke from off thy neck, and the yoke shall be destroyed because of the anointing."* (KJV) Our son accepted this assignment without hesitation. He always looked forward to spending time with his father, as my husband was very attentive to our son. As the weekend approached, he became quite ill. This caused some concern about the instruction God had given. However, Jason was a trooper, wanting to be with his Dad for the weekend, and being obedient to God's calling. Our son called me later the next day, said that he was sick all night, and could not keep anything down. However, he was determined to complete the task his Lord had given him. I felt a total peace in my spirit that God had His way in spite of the devil's attempt to destroy God's plan of deliverance.

Time to Move

As we waited for the manifestation of God's work, I diligently sought God about moving. I went to my Pastor for counsel, and he suggested the church apartments. That sounded wonderful, because I knew those apartments were under the protected covering of Jesus. They are also right on the school and church grounds where I worked and attended services. In addition, another benefit of being close by was that I did not have a dependable vehicle at the time. I loved the thought of living where God's presence dwells; it is so peaceful!

It was all settled and scheduled, our son and I would be moving the first week in March of 1996. It would be the first time in approximately a year and a half we would have our own place to live. True joy and happiness filled my soul for the first time in over five years! There was a release in my spirit . . . this most difficult assignment was almost over. We moved the first week in March, and my beloved was home two months later. On July 7, 1996, my husband rededicated his life to his Lord and Savior Jesus Christ. He has continued to serve God faithfully with his whole heart, upholding the infallible Word of God.

Chapter Seven - The Final Word

In Review

Dear reader, I have shared the most intimate, personal pieces of my heart with you. This is not because I wish to have someone's sympathy, it is simply my heartfelt desire to please my Lord Jesus and be of help to those in need of answers. I have written of the years and the tears that were most heart wrenching. I must tell you those years were also some of the dearest times with my Lord and Savior. During this most difficult time, I learned many things that have proven to enrich my life. I had a need that only Jesus could meet. Because of spending many sleepless nights praying, I developed a hunger to be in His presence. I began praying from the moment I opened my eyes in the morning and continued until I nodded off to sleep that night. I cannot emphasize it enough! This is where I found the strength, peace, and encouragement I desperately needed!

I learned that attending church services, even when I did not feel like it, was the right decision. It did not matter if I felt physically or emotionally drained, each time I went, the Holy Spirit gave me encouragement and strength that built my faith. Jesus is a friend that sticks closer than a brother! I am praying that you will turn to our Lord and Savior Jesus Christ with your troubles and fears, no matter how big or small. God's phone number is Jeremiah 33:3,

"Call to me, and I will answer you. I will tell you great and mysterious things that you do not know."

A word of caution . . . when you become tired of waiting on answers to prayer, it is imperative that you continue to wait! Hang on for as long as it takes, DO NOT GIVE UP! I am convinced this is the primary reason why Christians do not receive answers to their prayers. They become weak and impatient, and as a result, they lose faith. It is vital to your spiritual health to find a church with a preacher that preaches and teaches the Word of God.

Our Lord God is never late and He does not lie, so we must learn to trust and wait. Our Lord never gave up on any of us . . . He patiently waits for us; therefore, we must not give up. *"No one has ever heard, no one has paid attention, and no one has seen any god except you. You help those who wait for you."* (Isaiah 64:4)

If You Need a Miracle

If you do not know Jesus as your personal Savior, and you have a desire to see God perform a miracle in your life, I invite you to pray the following prayer:

> *Father, I know that I have broken your laws and my sins have separated me from you. I am truly sorry, please forgive me, and help me avoid sinning again. I believe that Jesus Christ died for my sins. I believe that He was resurrected from the dead. I invite Jesus to become the Lord of my life, to rule and reign*

in my heart from this day forward. Please send
your Holy Spirit to help me obey You, and to do
Your will for the rest of my life. In Jesus' name
I pray, Amen.

If you once knew Jesus Christ as your personal Savior, but are not serving God in the way you should, I strongly encourage you to rededicate your life to Him. He is patiently waiting to do a work in your life.

"However, when God our Savior made his
kindness and love for humanity appear, he saved us,
but not because of anything we had done to gain his
approval. Instead, because of his mercy he saved us
through the washing in which the Holy Spirit gives us
new birth and renewal." (Titus 3:4–5)

An Unexpected Phone Call

At this time, I would like to speak of an opportunity the Lord gave me to share Jesus. The phone rang one Saturday afternoon. I answered the phone not expecting to hear this voice on the other end. It was the woman my husband had been with for several months. At first, I was stricken with fear! Why is she calling . . . what do I say . . . how am I supposed to react . . . should I be kind . . . or give her a piece of my mind? Questions and more questions flooded my mind. She just wanted to talk to the wife of the man who had been with her. She opened her heart, saying she did not mean to hurt me, and she was sorry for all the pain she had caused me and my family. This shocked me! This is unheard of . . . I did not have a choice, for my heart began to melt with tears, among somewhat mixed feelings. After five or ten minutes, I began sharing Jesus with her. I was not sure how she would receive this. As the conversation went on, she was very receptive. I answered her questions to the best of my ability, and then I asked her if we could pray. My heart has forever been touched through this woman's thoughtful and sincere words. After 30–40 minutes, we hung up. I could not believe what I just heard . . . I just cried and cried. The Lord truly worked a miracle of healing, compassion, and love in me toward this woman. (If this woman is reading this, your compassion has left a mark on my heart. I prayed for you before our phone call and I will always have a special place in my heart for you. Jeremiah 29:11)

The Road of Life

At first, I saw God as my observer, my judge, keeping track of the things I did wrong, so as to know whether I merited heaven or hell when I die. He was out there sort of like a president. I recognized His picture when I saw it, but I really didn't know Him.

But later on when I met Christ, it seemed as though life were rather like a bike ride, but it was a tandem bike, and I noticed that Christ was in the back helping me pedal.

I don't know just when it was that He suggested we change places, but life has not been the same since. When I had control, I knew the way. It was rather boring, but predictable . . . It was the shortest distance between two points.

But when He took the lead He knows the delightful long cuts, up mountains, and through rocky places at breakneck speeds, it was all I could do to hang on! Even though it looked like madness, He said, "Pedal!"

I worried and was anxious and asked, "Where are you taking me?" He laughed and didn't answer, and I started to learn to trust. I forgot my boring life and entered into the adventure. And when I'd say, "I'm scared," He'd lean back and touch my hand.

He took me to people with gifts that I needed. Gifts of healing, acceptance, and joy. They gave me gifts to take on my journey, My Lord's and mine.

And we're off again. He said, "Give the gifts away; they're extra baggage, too much weight." So I did, to the people we met, and I found that in giving I received, and still our burden was light.

I did not trust Him at first, to be in control of my life. I thought He'd wreck it; but He knows bike secrets, knows how to make it bend to take sharp corners, knows how to jump to clear high rocks, and knows how to fly to shorten scary passages.

And I am learning to shut up and pedal in the strangest places, and I'm beginning to enjoy the view and the cool breeze on my face with my delightful constant companion, Jesus Christ.

And when I'm sure I just can't do anymore, He just smiles and says . . ."Pedal."

Author Unknown

The Restoration

My husband and I have been enjoying the gift

of God's faithfulness in our family for over nine years now. Our three children have experienced the blessings of God. They are doing well. They have witnessed the tender, yet mighty Hand of God. This has strengthened their walk and bolstered their faith. They have seen God work miracles of healing and restoration.

The Lord has blessed our family with two grandchildren, with one more on the way. Children are a gift from God, while grandchildren are rewards. I share a psalm of praise with you, *"A psalm of praise. Of David. I will exalt you, my God the King; I will praise your name for ever and ever. Every day I will praise you and extol your name for ever and ever. Great is the LORD and most worthy of praise; his greatness no one can fathom. One generation will commend your works to another; they will tell of your mighty acts. They will speak of the glorious splendor of your majesty, and I will meditate on your wonderful works. They will tell of the power of your awesome works, and I will proclaim your great deeds. They will celebrate your abundant goodness and joyfully sing of your righteousness. The LORD is gracious and compassionate, slow to anger and rich in love. The LORD is good to all; he has compassion on all he has made. All you have made will praise you, O LORD; your saints will extol you."* (Psalms 145:1–10, NIV)

Before closing the final chapter of this book, I must make mention of the precious spiritual warriors of my home church, Phoenix Christian Assembly. I know of many that lifted our family before the Lord daily. A few made sacrifices through fasting and prayer. Without a doubt, these believers touched the throne of God for their friends. God looks favorably on Christians such as these. He teaches us in Galatians 6:1–2, *"Brothers and sisters, if a person gets trapped by wrongdoing, those of you who are spiritual should help that person turn away from doing wrong. Do it in a gentle way. At the same time watch yourself so that you also are not tempted. Help carry each other's burdens. In this way you will follow Christ's teachings."*

Our Pastor has taught us to stand on God's word and to exercise our faith. According to Hebrews 11:6, without faith it is impossible to please God. Jesus Himself told us in Matthew 17:20, *"He told them, Because you have so little faith. I can guarantee this truth: If your faith is the size of a mustard seed, you can say to this mountain, 'Move from here to there,' and it will move. Nothing will be impossible for you."*

Without the prayers of these faithful prayer warriors, God's grace and favor may not have been experienced in such a powerful way. I thank you, my faithful friends . . . from the bottom of my heart. A special thanks to our Pastor and his wife for the teaching and preaching of the infallible Word of God. Your love and prayers mean more than any words can express.

The author with her husband in October of 2004.

Contact Shelley K. Reichenbach
or order more copies of this book at

TATE PUBLISHING, LLC

127 East Trade Center Terrace
Mustang, Oklahoma 73064

(888) 361 - 9473

Tate Publishing, LLC

www.tatepublishing.com